CONFI-DANCE

Memoirs of an Asian businesswoman's journey from a
traditional upbringing into unconditional love

By
May Lam Rocco

CONTENTS

Foreword **5**

Introduction **8**

Chapter 1 Heritage and Childhood 10

Chapter 2 New Countries and Moves into Independence 42

Chapter 3 A Marriage of Two Families 77

Chapter 4 The Denial 103

Chapter 5 The Breakup of Two Families 125

Chapter 6 Depression 142

Chapter 7 A New Beginning 169

Chapter 8 Unconditional Love 181

Chapter 9 Reflections on the Journey 188

Acknowledgments **205**

About the Author **207**

Notes in Closing **208**

To Albert

I have written this book for you—to share my life journey, and through my experience, to let you know that no matter what happens to you, it is happening for you. I am very proud of who you have become and I know you will always find your way. I love you unconditionally. Thank you for teaching me so much about being a good parent.

To those who doubt their ability to overcome challenges in life

I believe "where there is a will, there is a way." I hope my story shines a light on all that is possible with our life, whether it is a desire to pursue what we want or to have the love and joy of that special relationship with our children. Every one of us deserves to be happy and to live our life fully.

FOREWORD

*C*onfi-Dance is a book with lessons for everyone. May Lam Rocco takes us on her journey, but it is also easy to see our own journeys in her story. May shares with transparency, vulnerability, and wisdom. From her childhood as part of a traditional Chinese family, through the years of pursuing the approval of others, to discovering the power of unconditional love, she has written a beautiful, painful, and hopeful story of personal growth.

I first met May in August 2009. My son, Jesse, who was living in Shanghai, thought that May and I would connect well with each other. He thought she may be a good business partner for a psychometrics business I was contemplating building in greater China. We started working together as strategic partners and then decided to merge our businesses in 2012. We continued to work closely until I retired from our business in December 2018. During those nine years, May proved herself wise, tenacious, and competent time and again as our managing partner. With the help of a wonderful home-office team, we were able to train and certify over one thousand coaches, trainers, and HR professionals across greater China who continue to make a difference in the lives of others today. After serving people in Asia for over thirty years, the nine years we worked together as business partners created many of my greatest memories. In addition, May and her husband, Frank, have become wonderful lifelong friends whom I cherish.

However, even if I didn't know May personally, this book would have been engaging, instructive, and often heart-wrenching. She shares her story with such clarity and reflection that it will be hard for you to read it without seeing personal applications. Have you ever found yourself diminishing your own values to please someone else? Have you contemplated making tough decisions, not knowing where they will lead? Have you ever gone through a crisis of confidence that tore at the core of your self-image? Are you estranged from your parents or children, not knowing how to repair the damage? You will find all these experiences shared with a humble rawness in this book. But you will also discover the way out into a beautiful future. With wisdom that only comes through personal evaluation and change, May writes about her own joys and pains, and the decisions she has made that were harmful, but also those that gave her a better way forward. Finally, she recognizes the redemptive benefits in every experience and how they have made her the person she is today. She gives us the precious gift of knowing her deeply through her writing while also giving us hope for our own lives and relationships.

This book is one I will read and re-read because of the way it connects the heart and the head to a life that is worth living.

Ron Price

President, TTI Success Insights

INTRODUCTION

This is a wonderful story about a modern Chinese woman's life and development in free-world Asia. Born in Hong Kong to a strong-willed patriarchal family of relatively modest means, May writes of her emergence from a happy but modest childhood through gainful apprenticeship to her entrepreneurially successful father, combined with superb educational opportunities in Asia and later in London, followed by her own early business success.

Had it ended there, May's story would simply have been a tale of living "happily ever after." Life is not always quite so easy, and May soon confronted hurdles that have destroyed lesser women . . . and men.

Chinese culture is still not accustomed to successful women. The strictures of conventional life can hamstring an enterprising lady. When lured into a marriage for the benefit of her new father-in-law, May had every reason to believe in happy endings. She was immediately disillusioned by an unloving and dissolute husband who left her utterly devoid of love and happiness apart from the arrival of her only child several years into the marriage.

Divorce cost May her business and her familial relationships with both in-laws and even her own family. She was left with virtually no emotional nor financial support from anyone other than her own steel will and the love of her young son, Albert. But May Lam was a strong and capable woman. Her story capitalizes on her good fortune to acquire lasting friends who cared for her, a rise back to financial success built on her own achievement and no other, and an introduction to Frank Rocco, a successful American attorney, a truly loving man who with her son, Albert, became the center of her life.

May Lam Rocco is an independent woman, a successful woman, and an inspiration to women around the world. Her story is valuable in any culture.

Bob Livingston

Speaker-elect of the US House of Representatives

Chapter 1

HERITAGE AND CHILDHOOD

When growing up, I never knew what it meant to want something. To have a preference for one thing over another.

No one in my family ever asked me what I wanted. Whatever was given to me—to eat, to wear, to do, to grow up and be—that was what it was supposed to be. Without question. We were a typical big Chinese family and that was simply how it worked.

We were Chinese, but we didn't make our home in China. My family made other choices that took them away from what they had first known.

And eventually, after many years, I learned to as well.

My father was born in 1933 in Kuala Lumpur, the capital of Malaysia, to my grandparents, Lim Yook Fai and Cheung Yook Moy. As the story goes, when my father and his brothers were very young, my grandfather was kidnapped by local bandits—one of whom was his best friend—and taken to a small hut in the middle of the jungle. The family owned a number of businesses along with a rubber plantation and was considered well off. Because of this, the bandits demanded a huge ransom for my grandfather's return—one million Malaysian ringgit, which was an incredible amount of money at that time.

Everyone in the family was scared and didn't know what to do, especially since Grandpa was the oldest son and the head of the family. They were afraid to go to the police because they knew if they did, Grandpa would have been killed.

While the family was trying to gather the ransom money, Grandpa suddenly returned home unharmed, telling my grandma he found a gun in his cell where he was locked up and used it to shoot the man watching over him that night. He then took the key to free himself and escaped, unsure of whether the guard was still alive or dead. When he returned home, he no longer felt safe, perhaps in part because his friend, who knew many details of his life there, was a part of the kidnapping. He quickly gathered his whole family and left Kuala Lumpur in the middle of the night.

First, they went to Malacca, about ninety miles away, which in those days was considered very far. They stayed with their relatives for about a year, but Grandpa still didn't think it was a safe place for him and his family. He then moved everyone to Singapore for a while before finally landing in Hong Kong to live with relatives.

Grandpa was an entrepreneur; soon after he settled the family in Hong Kong, he went to Guangzhou, China, and bought a few buses to start a transportation business. Then he moved the whole family to China.

When my father was old enough, he began to help with the business, learning how to fix the bus tires and service the engines. Then when China gained independence in 1949 and the People's Republic of China was formed, the business climate became more unstable, which affected my grandpa's transportation company. For a short time, my grandpa continued the business, going down to just one bus. When my father turned seventeen, he got his driving license so he could help drive the bus as well.

He saw his father working so hard and yet the business still barely brought in enough money to feed the whole family. And as political change slowly came over the country, he knew it would only get harder. He needed to find something else.

One day, my father saw an opportunity and he took it. With some of their hard-earned money, he went to Guangdong to set up a small tire-repair shop in a busy junction where buses, trucks, and cars had to pass through on their way to most of the major cities. He'd seen the opportunity while driving the bus, noticing how many trucks and army cars needed to pass through and realizing many of their tires would need repair after long hours driving on sandy or muddy roads. It was also a place where the drivers could take a break before going off to their next destination. When drivers and soldiers stopped, my father would offer clean water, biscuits, and beers, and because of his friendliness, they liked him. Business was good and he made his first bucket of money. This business didn't last long, though, as it was also soon taken over by the government.

Soon after, my grandfather went back to Malaysia to sell the family rubber plantation and move most of the family back to Hong Kong, starting a new business out of a shop house. Meanwhile, my father went to Hainan, a small island in the smallest and southernmost province of China. There, he began to work as a driver for the army. Eventually, he got to drive for an army general, which gave him benefits such as better food and housing. The general was very fond of him and advised him to leave China to seek better opportunities. My father took this advice.

But before he left, something else happened that greatly shaped his life. He met my mother.

My parents when they first met - Hainan, China, 1954

My mother was born in Hainan, China, in 1937.

My grandma swore by eating raw sesame during pregnancy, to make the baby's skin flawless. She told me many times when she was alive, "Remember—eat the white sesame, your baby will have beautiful skin." And her baby daughter did. Because she had this beautiful skin, she stood out and was considered adorable by many people in the village. Grandma was a very clean and tidy person, and although she didn't have much, she made sure my mother always had clean clothes to wear and looked tidy.

One day during the Japanese occupation, when my mother was three years old, she was lining up in the street to get food from the army like most of the kids in the village. As she stood there, a convoy of Japanese cars and trucks drove past and suddenly a big, beautiful sedan stopped. A Japanese woman got out of the car, picked her up, and drove off.

The news quickly passed to my grandma, who was working nearby. She quickly went to the Japanese general's office to beg for the return of her daughter.

It turned out the woman was the general's wife, who told my grandma that she really liked my mother and wanted permission for her to stay at their house. The general's wife promised she would raise her as her own and my grandmother could come and visit her anytime she wanted. Grandma didn't have much choice under the circumstances except to agree, because she didn't want to offend the Japanese.

My mother later described to me her memories of that time with the general and his wife. She didn't talk about how leaving her mother affected her emotionally, but she did talk about how she was treated really well while she was with them. They dressed her in beautiful clothes and took her out in their fancy car to different places, holding her hands as if she was their own child.

She stayed with them for a few years until the general and his family had to leave Hainan. Before the family left, they asked my grandma if they could take my mother back to Japan. But my grandma begged them to return my mother to her and my grandfather—she was their only child and all they had—and eventually they agreed.

So my mother was returned to my grandma.

My grandfather had gone to work in Singapore as an accountant when my mother was born, and when he returned to Hainan, my mother was seven years old. He asked her if she could speak English, and when my mother said no, he began to teach her by using a phonetic alphabet. But before long, he passed away. My mother never got a chance to learn English or know him well.

She later described him to me as a tall, slender, handsome man, from whom I got my looks. She said he spoke gently and spoke English very well.

The rumor was that he got the black magic in the boat when he returned from Singapore, from a woman there who liked my grandpa and asked him not to leave. Grandpa had told her he had a wife and a daughter in China waiting for his return and left to come back to China to be reunited with them.

My mother was considered a good student at school, which in those days in China meant you needed excellence academically, in health (exercising often), and mentally (to listen to the government). She achieved all three things. She had beautiful Chinese handwriting; I was told she taught my father's younger brother how to write when he was young. My second brother, Barry, also picked up his writing skill from her—he has beautiful handwriting too.

She had high standards for herself, something that was always clear to me growing up. She told me how she was determined to be the best and worked hard at whatever she did. She read a lot and understood the economic and political scene. She often shared with me a world perspective and advised me how to be strong in adversity and kind to others.

Her marriage to my father was a good example of her determination.

When she turned seventeen, the age of marriage in her time, Grandma asked the matchmaker to introduce her to suitors like doctors and merchants in the village. But my mother wasn't interested in anyone until she met my father.

I once asked her, "Why didn't you marry a doctor or merchant in China? Why instead did you marry a foreigner, like Dad?"

She told me she wanted to get out of China. In her mind, China was too closed off. She knew there was another world out there. This might have something to do with the time she spent with the Japanese general's family at a young age, which let her see the possibility of having a different life.

My father was able to give her that opportunity. I sometimes wondered, was there real love in my parents' relationship when they met? Or just a way for her to escape from China?

Once they were married, they left China with the intent to reunite with my father's family. First, though, they needed to spend a year in the Portuguese colony of Macau, while my mother waited for visa approval. Once it came, they moved to Hong Kong.

Mom and Dad when they moved to live in Hong Kong - 1956

My brothers and I were born in Hong Kong, in the Yau Ma Tei district in the Kowloon Peninsula, and for the first six years of my life lived there with my family in a shop house.

There were eighteen of us altogether in that house— my great-grandma and three grandparents on my father's side (my grandfather had two wives), uncles and aunts, cousins, my grandma on my mother's side, my three brothers and me, and my parents.

In that generation, it wasn't common for a mother to live with her daughter after she married. In the Chinese custom, parents would live with the son and his family, since a daughter was considered married off to another family. Her last name would change and their children would carry their husband's family name. But when my father had brought my mother to Hong Kong to join his family, my grandmother had joined them. My father's father asked her to come, and when she did, she became a big part of my and my brothers' lives.

The ground floor held our kitchen, but mostly functioned as a showroom and warehouse for our family business. It was always greasy, with buckets of gasoline and grease set out to use for the engine parts we sold. I didn't like the presence of either; I could smell the gasoline when I walked downstairs and the grease looked dirty to me.

Upstairs was where we lived and slept. I shared the floor with my siblings, cousins, and my grandmother on my mom's side, while the rest of the adults slept in a makeshift bedroom made by drawing a curtain around their bed at night. There were only two small windows for light to come in. Most of the time, it was dark.

My family owned a business, we owned a car, and we had food on the table every day, but we were not like rich people who could buy whatever they wanted. I was too young to understand the differences in classes, but I knew we never went hungry.

My father was constantly travelling for business—I hardly saw him when I was young—and my mother was always busy cooking and cleaning, taking care of all eighteen people. She did a lot, for all of us. In the morning, I saw her in the front shop helping Grandpa with the business, then in the afternoon she and her mother would be doing the cooking and other chores for the family. By the end of the day, she was always tired. I was too young to really understand why she had to cook for so many people. She never complained or talked about how she felt. While my mother was busy doing house chores, my grandma—her mother—would help out and also take care of us kids.

My brothers and I were free to run around the surrounding neighborhood, but we knew we shouldn't venture too far away. My mother told us it was dangerous, that some bad people would pick us up and sell us to another country.

One day, my brothers and I were playing in the street and there was a big white tent put up, with monks and other people inside. I heard chanting and people crying and saw a long table placed in the center of the tent with a big portrait of an elderly person. The table was also filled with fresh and dried fruits, cooked chicken and pork, small plastic glasses, and wine. Incense was burning, and occasionally the monk would pour wine onto the floor while chanting. The people inside the tent would do the same. They would pray, chant, bow, and cry. They also scattered the dried food and some five-cent coins onto the floor.

When we saw this, my brothers and I picked up the coins and ran as fast as we could to avoid being caught. We ran to the small convenience store at the back street of our shop house and used the coins to buy whatever we could get. I remember standing in front of the store for a long time, holding onto the money, trying to decide whether I should get an ice cream or an orange fizzy drink from the juice fountain. At the end, I settled for the orange fizzy drink and finished it fast. Then I regretted it, thinking I should have gotten the ice cream, to enjoy it longer.

When Mom found out we took the money from the street, she was angry and said we shouldn't have picked up the money. We told her it was on the street floor, that we weren't stealing. Mom then told us the money was meant for the dead people to use in the afterlife, and we were so scared thinking the dead people would come and haunt us. My mother always told us to be honest, not to steal or take things that didn't belong to us. This was how we learned.

At that age, we didn't have much, no dolls or toys to play with, but we didn't feel we lacked anything.

I remember one game my brothers and I played with the neighbor kids where we used six small square parcels sewed up with raw rice inside. We would take turns throwing one up in the air, reaching to grab more from the ground, and then catching the one we'd just thrown, all with just one hand. Whoever dropped the parcel would lose the game. We could play it all day long.

While we didn't have much, we were just happy kids.

When I was six years old, the whole family moved from the shop house to a high-rise apartment in the busiest street of Kowloon.

The business had been growing and my father had sent home the money to buy two apartments on Nathan Road, a street that stretched over 3.6 kilometers from one end to the other with many shops and restaurants on both sides.

All eighteen of us moved into the new apartment, which was about sixteen hundred square feet. My brothers and me, my grandma, and my parents all slept in one room, with my brothers occupying the top of our bunk bed, my mother and me sleeping on the bottom, and Grandma on the floor on a small futon. When my father came back from travelling, Grandma would move to the living room to sleep and I would sleep with one of my cousins so Mom and Dad could sleep in the lower bunk. In the mornings, Grandma would roll up the futon so we had a small space to put a folding table and chairs, which we used for our studies.

Grandma woke up very early in the morning and went to bed late, so we hardly saw the futon on the floor.

I don't have many memories of my dad in the room. He still travelled frequently in those days and mostly spent his time in Brunei.

I do have many memories of my grandma, mother, and brothers from that time.

Grandma continued to help take care of us, and as I was starting kindergarten that year, this then included making sure that we had clean clothes to wear, our school uniforms were well pressed, and our pencil cases always had sharpened pencils. She also took us to the bus stop in the morning and met us there again after school. Once in a while, my grandma would cook us some special food for lunch like putting eggs into the hot rice and mixing it up with soy sauce. It was so good. Other times, she would make us salty pork congee, and occasionally we would have roasted pork bought from a meat shop near our home. That was definitely a treat for us.

Our education was very important to our mother. She wanted us to study hard and learn how to speak English well. Before I began kindergarten, my mother had got up at 4 a.m. to line up in front of the Catholic school in Kowloon—not because she was religious but because it was a very prestigious school. She wanted to make sure I had the opportunity to study there.

And I did, for the first six years of my education. She did the same for my brothers, doing all she could to get them into good public schools that had limited spots for new students. That was my mother. She did her best with what she had, her standards were always high, and she knew education was the key to success. She was not afraid to ask, to find the resources she needed to give us the best she could provide, even though she didn't have much.

My brother Mike was the oldest of the four of us, and so he also did what he could to help take care of us. Being the oldest meant he had to take care of his brothers and sister, something my parents kept reminding him about. In Chinese culture, when the parents are no longer alive or even when they are in old age, the oldest son will take on the role of father and his wife will be the mother, taking care of the family including the younger siblings. Mike is a very traditional man, very obedient, and family has always been very important to him. He takes care of everyone much like my father does.

One year, my brother Barry got into trouble at school. I didn't know what kind of trouble he was in; all I knew was that he told my brother someone in school wanted to have trouble with him and he was scared. Mike was angry, quickly gathered a few of his friends, and headed to the school to straighten things out. I wasn't sure whether he got into a fight with them or just threatened something, but the next day, everything was fine with Barry. Even at that young age, he felt obligated to take care of his brother when he was in trouble. Even today, when we all have our own families, he still thinks it is his job to take care of us.

I remember how Mike loved to collect stamps. He would save all his pocket money to buy beautiful stamps and put them in custom-made stamp books. One time, I took some of his stamps and gave them to my classmates at school. When he found out, he was so angry—he told Mom about it and I got scolded. Mike was angry at me for a long time. At the time, I hadn't even known it was a wrong thing to do. All I knew was my classmates started to like me more—they kept asking me to have more of the stamps and they all wanted to play with me. It was a good feeling to be liked. Through this, I began to learn that pleasing others was a way to get attention, to get people to like me.

My second oldest brother, Barry, also enjoyed collecting and had a battlefield on top of his bunk bed that was full of little toy soldiers, tanks, and trucks atop a long piece of wood fixed to the wall. I used to climb up there to admire the soldiers. He would paint each one of them differently, some with green jackets and red pants, others with brown uniforms. Then he would arrange them in front of the tanks or sitting inside open-top trucks covered with green plastic brushes. He was always so patient—sometimes he would spend hours just doing that.

Little John, my youngest brother, was always quiet, observing others, speaking very softly, and seldom getting into trouble. When we were young, he would just tag along with us wherever we could take him, and when we asked him to do things for us, he was always willing to help and put on a nice smile. Because of his quietness, my parents thought he wasn't a smart kid. They thought if you acted fast—responded quickly when asked to do chores, for example—then you were smart. John does things his own way; he has a process to think things through. He is also a very responsible person and does things quietly without wanting any praise or acknowledgment from others. I loved all my brothers, and especially my younger brother John. I didn't think my parents were particularly fair in thinking he wasn't smart enough to handle certain things. I felt like I wanted to protect him. Deep down, I was sure it hurt him to feel a sense of my parents not treating him fairly. He probably wanted to make my parents proud like all kids do. Years later, when my mother and my grandma were getting old, they moved back to live in China. John and his family took care of them without question; he never complained, no matter how hard the situation was. He would accept everything as his duty.

The four of us had a good childhood together.

The family gave my mother a small amount of monthly pocket money to spend on us or small things that she needed. It wasn't much. To earn more, she and my grandma would get bags of toy clothes sewn together from the factories and separate them by cutting the threads on each piece. There were hundreds of little garments in each bag and they didn't bring in much—just one dollar per bag— but it was an extra income for my mother. My brothers and I would help out after we finished our homework. At night, our small living spaces would fill with bags and bags of these toy clothes and threads everywhere, as we worked to help finish whatever Mother got from the factory that day. If she said, "Oh, we can only get four bags today," we knew it would be an early night for us, taking just about two hours between the six of us. I knew part of the money was used for buying that special roast pork for our lunches, and part of it was to save for our future.

To save money, Mother also made my clothes when we were young, especially those meant for the Chinese New Year. She would stretch her money by picking up a piece of leftover odd-sized fabric from the shop, one they couldn't sell but could work to make a dress or a pair of trousers for a child. I still remember one Chinese New Year outfit she sewed for me—an ugly yellow jacket and pants. I didn't like it at all because it wasn't store-bought, but I could tell the materials were good. It lasted for years. I wore the same ugly yellow suit for Chinese New Year until I grew out of it and there was no more hem to let out.

My cousins who stayed in the same house would wear beautiful clothes that were bought from a store every year. I used to complain to my mother, asking why she didn't go to the shop to buy me a ready-made dress. She would say it was too expensive. But I wondered why my cousins could afford the new clothes and we all lived together as a family. Later on, I learned that my uncle was in charge of the family money, money that my father would send back to the family from Brunei or the money the family earned from the business. My father would trust his brother to take care of everyone in the family.

My mother never said anything about the unfairness; she just kept quiet. She wasn't from the same village and didn't speak the same Chinese dialects, which made certain things difficult. She was viewed as an outsider and additionally her communication with my father's mother was difficult at first—she had to learn my father's dialect to have a meaningful conversation. My uncle's wife spoke the same dialect and she was the favorite of my paternal grandma, perhaps because it was easier for them to talk to each other. For whatever reason, my grandma treated my mom differently.

It was a difficult time for my mother in the family, but she was a strong woman. She kept going.

When the family business became more successful, we bought our first black-and-white television. I was eight years old. I still remember the day my uncle brought home this huge box—everyone in the family gathered around the box to see what it was. When my uncle lifted it out of the box and placed it on top of the table, we just stared. There was a white screen with a black rim and two knots on the bottom. We wondered what it was. Once the TV was connected, we could see images of people and hear them talking. It was fascinating to us. Before the TV, we could only listen to the radio, mostly at night. I remember in particular one station of ghost storytelling. My grandma, my brothers, and I would gather around the radio, clinging to each other, terrified as the storyteller described the scene of the horror story. When it reached the climax, I would cover my ears and tuck my head into my grandma's chest. She kept saying it was only a story. And to this day, I don't like horror stories or movies. When we first got the TV, we would sit and watch all day after school, until my mother decided we would have to finish our homework first.

In those days, we each received a small amount of pocket money each month from my mother. I would use the money to buy plastic beads to make my own bracelets, necklaces, and rings. Other times, I would buy my favorite fruit when it was in season, a tropical fruit called longan. I was afraid to let anyone know I had it, because my mother always said we had to share or offer to the elderly in the family first. When I looked at my small bag of longan, which was only around twenty pieces, I knew that if I offered to share with the family, I would leave with nothing. So I decided not to and quietly climbed on top of the bunk bed, covered myself with a blanket, and enjoyed the fruit. Occasionally, I would share a few pieces with John and we both would stay covered with the blanket until all the longan was gone. It was satisfying but I also felt guilty at the same time because I knew I should offer it to other family members first.

This practice of offering first to others showed up in other ways, and did stay with me.

At our house in the high-rise apartment, we had a very big, folded round board that leaned against the wall, and when dinner time came, my mother and aunt would put it on top of a small table. When it was unfolded, it turned into a huge table that would seat sixteen to eighteen people, much like what you see in a Chinese restaurant. We would take it out only during mealtime, and then my whole family, all eighteen of us, would sit tightly together.

I would help set the table, placing the chopsticks, plates, rice bowls, and teacups, and filling the bowls with rice. My mother, grandma (on my mother's side), and aunt would then bring out the food from the kitchen—almost every night we would have chicken, fish, pork, soup, and vegetables. Then I would call my family to come for dinner. My young cousin and my brothers could smell the food. They came running to the table.

During the dinner, whenever I heard the sound of chopsticks touching the bowl, I would know it was time to stand up and fetch rice for the elderly. I was always the first one to stand up. I'm not sure why; maybe it was the attention that I was craving. I would also pour tea for everyone when I would see their empty teacup, sometimes doing it two to three times over the course of the meal.

It is a custom for the Chinese to have tea with their meal. It was also our custom to let the elders and men take their food first. For instance, if we were having chicken, the drumsticks and wings were considered the best part of the chicken and would be for my grandparents or uncle to take first. Then my mother and aunt would take theirs, and the children would take whatever was left behind, usually the chicken breast or the bony parts.

My mother taught me to take the food in front of me and not to choose or flip the food. When it came to fish, most often a big steamed fish, there often wasn't much left by the time it was my turn. I would eat the fish left on the bone or what fell into the sauce, mixing it with rice. I didn't mind at all—I thought it was more delicious and besides, I could eat more rice with it.

I have a number of happy memories of my mother.

Despite not having much, her standards remained high. She would design the house beautifully, using simple, inexpensive things. There were plants and flowers everywhere and it was always tidy and clean.

She dressed me very proper and taught me how to sit and behave like a lady. When the family business started to do well, we were financially better off. My mother would then pick out clothes for me from the stores, using her eye for beautiful things. She would often go to a shop not far from where we lived that sold mostly imported clothes from Japan, and buy during sales. She knew they were better quality and the design was different from the locally made clothes. The shop owner was kind to her, giving her very good prices even beyond the sale amount because she wore their dresses beautifully.

One time, the shop owner was trying to sell me a jacket from his store. My mom asked me to try it on, and when I did, the sleeves were too short. Unhappy to lose a sale, the owner told my mom I had a weird figure, that my arms were too long. I was around eleven or twelve years old.

I was considered tall for a Chinese girl my age, and had long arms and long legs. In school I sat at the back of the room. I was ashamed about my height. I thought I was weird looking, at least until I went to study in England,

and I saw that most of the English people were quite tall, too. I could fit into their clothes well, which helped me realize I was actually very normal.

She also helped us as we learned English. During the first few years of my education, my mother would learn how to speak English words and simple English sentences to then teach them to my brothers and me at home. I am still amused she would learn that just to teach us. Then when we were old enough to go to study in England, she took out all her savings to pay for the school fees and airline tickets for us. "You have to learn good English because it is important for your future," she said. That was her dream for us, to be successful.

One of my favorite memories with her was from my early teenage years, when she and I would go to the café together once in a while when she had the time. We just ordered iced coffee and nothing else; this was all we could afford, and we would stay there savoring it as long as we could. It came with a big layer of whipped cream on top and tasted so delicious. I always looked forward to going there. Even today, I still love coffee with whipped cream.

Going to a café was a very western thing for us to do at that time—most other customers were from a well-off family or western educated. My mother wouldn't tell anyone in the family that we went.

I could see how much she enjoyed being there, and she made a pretty picture in the setting. She was a very tidy person, and always had beautiful hair and was well-dressed despite the fact we didn't have much money. She also had a very nice figure, and so in everything she wore, she looked beautiful.

My beautiful and elegant mother - Hong Kong, 1964

One day, she took me to a photo studio, just the two of us. She made a beautiful white dress for me, like a princess dress, for the occasion. Even though I liked store-bought clothes best, I had to admit the dress was beautiful. She also let me wear her white plastic pearl necklace to go with it. The photographer asked me to stand in front of a backdrop of a garden scene and hold a long white plastic rose. "Smile," he said, and I happily obliged because I knew the photos would turn out beautiful. Then Mom joined me, and we took some more photos together. It's a fond memory.

I didn't see the photos until much later. Mom must have kept them quiet—she didn't let anyone know because she was afraid the family might not like it, or even question where the money came from.

She had a high standard for us in all we did, just as she did for herself.

If we didn't do well, we sure would hear it from her. When we did do well, we seldom received praise, but we could tell by her expression, if she just nodded or smiled, when she was pleased. My mother was afraid that if she praised us much, we would get big-headed and wouldn't try harder, so praise wasn't one of her strongest suits. It also wasn't in our traditional culture to praise kids either. Because of that, I grew up uncomfortable with it. When someone said nice things about me, I would feel shy and think I didn't deserve it.

Years later, Mom and I were out for dinner at a restaurant in Hong Kong, and she told me for the first time in my life how much she appreciated what I did for her. She told me I had taken her out to all these beautiful restaurants, taken her to many countries around the world, and if it wasn't for me, she would not have the chance to experience life. I was in tears and cried for a long time. I would never have thought I would hear her telling me this. Even today, each time I think of this, it brings tears to my eyes.

While my mother didn't often praise, she had a very kind heart. Every year when she lived in Hong Kong, she would either donate money or buy food and essential things for the senior home. First, she called to see what they needed—things like rice, milk powder, cookies, blankets, and diapers. Then she would go to the supermarket to purchase them and send them over. She usually felt that would be better than just giving out money. I don't think she trusted that the administration office would put the money to good use. So she preferred to handle it herself, and she did every year.

I remember another time at the ladies' room in a hotel in Hong Kong. After cleaning our hands, an older lady handed a small towel to us and my mother reached into her pocketbook and took out HK $200 ($25 USD) to give to the woman. In Hong Kong, most people would give HK $2 (25 cents USD) or at most HK $5 (50 cents USD) as tips for the service. I asked her why she gave so much, and she said, "She is old, she still has to work."

One other time, she saw another old lady pushing a big cart full of boxes and trash up the hill of a steep road in central Hong Kong. The old lady was pushing very slowly. Clearly you could tell her fragile body was not strong enough. My mother told me she would go to help her out, but I told her the old lady might think she was crazy and I stopped her from doing it. Looking back, I think I was embarrassed at the thought of her going and pushing the cart for the old lady, but not my mother.

Her kindness has taught me so much about how to treat others who are less fortunate than us. Sometimes I would cry just listening to the news of disasters that happened, or when life was lost due to tragedy. Then and now, it makes me feel sad, and I wonder about the unfairness of it all and why we can't live together as one.

My mother and I had occasional friction too, especially as I grew older and friends became a more important part of my life. I remember once when I was thirteen I wanted to go out to an apartment party in Hong Kong. It was a party that began while still light, at six o'clock, and there would be newspapers covering the windows to make it dark, and furniture would be pushed aside to create a dance floor. I thought going to a party with my friends seemed really cool and it meant a lot to me. I wanted to be part of the group, to be accepted. But when I asked my mother permission to go, she said no without any hesitation. I kept asking her why I couldn't go, persisting, and even throwing a tantrum like a little kid. "Why can't I go, Mom?" I kept asking. "I promise to be back by ten." She eventually got so angry that she slapped me on the face, and I ran out of the house and swore I wouldn't come back. I was angry, hurt, and humiliated—it was the first time my mother slapped me like that. In the past when she was angry when I did something wrong, she had hit me on my hand or leg but never on my face. And also in those other times, I had felt I had deserved it. This time I felt different. I hadn't done anything wrong. I just wanted to go out with my friends.

It wasn't so much the physical pain that hurt the most, but the feelings of unfairness that I couldn't understand. I circled around the apartment neighborhood for about an hour until my grandmother came to look for me. I still insisted I would not go back to the house.

I sat in the building management office until dark and Grandma sat there with me. She kept telling me that my mother didn't mean to hit me, that she was just tired. I continued sobbing, trying to justify to my grandma that my mother was wrong. I felt treated unfairly, and I felt like the next time I was invited to go to a party or hang out with friends, I wouldn't ask for permission. After that, I was sometimes rebellious. At the same time, I was always careful with people—when something wasn't comfortable to me, I wouldn't do it.

Life continued on, though, mostly in peace, in ways that generally centered on all the daily things, like school and meals, being at home and out with friends.

And then we made a big change.

Chapter 2

NEW COUNTRIES AND MOVES INTO INDEPENDENCE

In 1974, at age fourteen, I left Hong Kong for Brunei, a small country in Borneo with a population of two hundred thousand. Some of my family members, including my brothers Mike and John, had already left Hong Kong a few months earlier. I was travelling with my uncle and it was my first time taking a plane.

When we boarded, my uncle let me take the window seat so I could see the view outside. When the plane eventually took off, I could feel my body being pulled back by the force of the engine's power. I looked out the window and saw everything was moving away as we were lifted up to the sky. My uncle leaned over and asked me, "How do you feel? Isn't it fun?"

I didn't have the excitement I was hoping for, but it was an interesting feeling.

The whole journey was around three hours, and once we were up in the sky, I became fascinated by the view of white clouds floating outside the window. The beauty of the clouds was so soft and free, I wished I could touch them with my own hands. That feeling of freedom—I wondered how it felt.

When we began to approach the capital of Brunei, Bandar Seri Begawan, I could see vast areas of green land, trees, and forest below. It was beautiful. I had never seen a forest or so many trees before. Coming from a city like Hong Kong, where most of the areas were occupied by high-rise buildings, roads, and people, this was definitely a change for me.

When we landed, Dad was waiting at the airport. I could see him from the plane window—he was waving, excited to see the plane approaching the terminal. As soon as I stepped out of the plane, I could see him in the building, calling my name. Then when I walked down the steps out of the airplane and into the small terminal, immigration officers sitting and waiting to stamp our passports, I could see my dad again, smiling and waving behind them.

I heard him speaking the local language of Malay to the officers, like they were old friends. Although I didn't know what he was saying, I knew he was telling the officer I was his daughter, and I came from Hong Kong. The officer smiled at me when we approached and waved me to exit without even looking at our bags.

The new place was a bit of a shock for me coming from Hong Kong—it felt primitive but also somehow fresh and free. I didn't miss Hong Kong or my old school friends that much. Instead, I felt a sense of excitement to be in a different country, to see different scenery, to be with my family and especially with Dad. I hadn't realized how much I'd missed him until I saw him again.

It was no surprise that once again, in this new place, we were all staying together in one big house. What was different this time, though, was that the landlord, a local Malay, lived with his family on the second floor of the house. My father took me to visit them as soon as I arrived.

I noticed that the way the landlord and his wife dressed was very different from people in Hong Kong. Both would wear a long sarong wrapped around their waists, with the difference between them mostly the top piece and pattern. His wife would wear a long-sleeve cardigan or shirt that came down to hip length and he would wear an open buttoned shirt. Other customs were different there too.

When we entered a room, we would take off our shoes and walk with our bare feet. In Hong Kong, we would take off our shoes as well but then put on slippers to walk around the house. But in Brunei, people walked around without any footwear; their floors were always clean.

The landlord and his wife were very nice people. Although I couldn't understand everything they said in Malay, I could tell by the way they talked to my father, and occasionally, they would come to me and say something with a big smile on their face. I would smile back politely without knowing what they'd said.

I was amazed how Dad could speak so many languages. He was always good with people and very friendly, with the valuable skill of making people feel comfortable around him. Through his many years in business, he received a lot of help from his friends and customers. He's a very trustworthy person, never took people for granted, and always kept his word. That's what made him successful even in a totally strange country. I admired him for that and am thankful that he taught me those values, which became a part of my own way of doing business.

Later that year, my brother Barry, mother, and grandma joined us in Brunei. Once again, we had all eighteen of us staying under one roof.

My brothers and I attended a local school, St. Andrew's School, where we instantly became the most popular kids, simply because we were from Hong Kong, a big cosmopolitan city. We dressed differently, more fashionably, and our schoolmates all wanted to be our friends. They wanted to know from us what the modern world looked like, what the fashion trends were, and what we did in our free time. I had never had so much attention at school, and it was refreshing.

Mike soon became the head of the sport team, Barry was popular because of his good looks, and I was becoming one of the girls whom boys wanted to be friends with. John was quiet as usual, but he was well liked by our friends and his classmates. In Brunei, my brothers and I became closer, much closer than we were during our time in Hong Kong. We did almost everything together, at school and at home.

Then one day when we got home from school, Mom told us we were moving to a new flat, with only our family.

We were overjoyed by the news. It meant we would have our own house, just us, Mom and Dad, and Grandma.

My brothers and I went to see the flat, which had two bedrooms, a living room, a bathroom, and a kitchen. It wasn't very big, but we didn't care. This was the first time in our lives we would all be together, just us. It was perfect.

The apartment needed some fresh paint, so after school Mike gathered his friends, bought paint, and started painting. It was fun, and we were so happy. It was a special moment for us, and I knew it meant so much to my mother. Finally she had a home, her own home.

When we first moved in, we had very little furniture, just a bunk bed in one room and one bed in the other. Mom only had one rice cooker, no pots and pans or gas stove, but she was able to use one rice cooker to cook three dishes along with the rice for our first dinner. That night was the first time our family of seven ate together as one family. I felt a closeness to my parents, brothers, and grandma that night that I'd never felt before. It was a wonderful feeling I'll never forget.

Sitting in our first home in Brunei wearing
my school uniform - 1974

Life in Brunei was different from Hong Kong for many reasons. Because of the country's Muslim religion, there were only a few high-rise buildings—the highest was ten stories—since no structure could be higher than the national mosque. There were many mosques around, and every Friday afternoon the local Muslim people gathered inside and prayed. The sound of the prayers would travel to almost every corner of the city. It was a calming and beautiful sound, something I had never before experienced.

A large portion of our time, especially over the weekend, was spent at my father's quarry and construction business. The quarry was full of piles and piles of stones in different sizes, and trucks would come and park next to them. Then another machine with a bucket would fill the truck with stones and the truck would drive away. Another one would follow. Some days, I could see many trucks lined up at the entrance of the quarry waiting to get their supply. Then, I knew business was good for my father.

During the holiday time, my dad would take my brothers and me to the quarry, where we would walk around the site or sit at the office watching people work. There were workers coming in and out of the office constantly, bringing papers for the clerks to stamp. Later, I found out these were the truck drivers, and the stamps were to prove that they had received the stones so we could invoice the government or the clients. Dad told me this was how business was done: we made money to pay salaries, business expenses, and the license fee as the quarry operator.

He would take me to meet with all kinds of people—those in government offices, bankers, and executives from

Shell, which was one of our biggest customers at that time. I loved doing business—it fascinated me how it was conducted. And I was never afraid to go meet with people, no matter what position they held in their company. The experiences I had beginning at age six or seven continuing up through those in Brunei formed a foundation of my understanding of business, and helped me so much when I went into the business world myself.

Beyond this time spent at the business, we spent a lot of time together as a family. The culture in Brunei was very family oriented, and given the small population, there weren't many big shopping malls, movie theaters, restaurants, or shopping streets to walk for miles like in Hong Kong. We spent most of our time doing activities with our family and friends at home. We would go to friends' houses and they would visit us too.

In Hong Kong, we had all been so busy with our individual lives. We could only do so much together, and it usually ended up being just a couple of outings or picnics during the year, usually at Chinese New Year time. When we moved to Brunei, this changed.

My brothers and I would hang out together with our school friends, and we all had breakfast, lunch, and dinner as a family almost every day. Mom and Dad would take us out for meals in nice restaurants. And once every few months, my parents would take us to Singapore or Thailand or the Philippines for the weekend. There were also times that my father and I would go on a trip, just the two of us.

We would spend our time shopping, eating the local food, and hanging out in the swimming pool together. The trips always felt special because they were such quality time with him, which I never had in Hong Kong. They felt memorable too. During one trip to Singapore, I remember Dad taking me to a dress shop and asking the saleslady to help me pick out two beautiful dresses. To this day, I still remember how they looked.

This memory is still vivid for me not because of the dresses, but because of the love that I felt from him, that I hadn't felt before. It was an incredibly special moment for me.

School in Brunei wasn't as challenging as in Hong Kong, and this paired with our popularity made school even more enjoyable. There, we made new friends and learned new languages. The other students were mostly Chinese students who spoke different dialects, mostly Mandarin or Hokkien. The classes were all conducted in English, but there was a Malay language class too. Since we spoke Cantonese at home, these languages were all foreign to us, but as we were young, we picked them up quite fast. At least, I picked up on understanding them fast; speaking them didn't come as easily or quickly. Mike had the best language skill of all of us, and was starting to speak simple Malay less than a year after we arrived. I could only say a few simple words by then, but could usually get the meaning of what someone was saying if I knew the subject they were talking about.

After-school sports activities were a big part of our lives in Brunei. For me, it was swimming—my mother enrolled me in after-school lessons and I practiced every day for the swimming exam. It was a multilevel test, and I completed the bronze, silver, and gold levels. As part of the exam, I had to compete with myself by swimming laps in the Olympic-size pool within a certain time. That meant I got to practice swimming laps every day instead of just having fun.

I resisted it at first but my mother just became more persistent, and finally I got used to it and began to enjoy it. The bronze and silver levels were easy for me, but the gold had its challenges. I had to first jump from a two-story platform into the pool, then swim two laps with clothes and shoes on. After that, I took off my shoes and used my pants to make a float to rest for a minute before I began twenty-two laps of nonstop swimming. All of which I had to complete in half an hour.

The swimming wasn't too difficult for me but the jump down was hard. When I stood on the platform, my legs started to shake and my knees were weak. I just closed my eyes and jumped down. Then, I had no time to think or feel afraid—I just started to swim to complete the twenty-two laps within the time required.

When it was over, I felt deep joy in my heart, the feeling of accomplishing something big. I was so proud of myself. It was my first achievement like that, one I should have celebrated, jumping up and down, to express the joy of my success, but I didn't because I didn't know how to. It would feel odd to do that, or even express how I was feeling more quietly, in front of others without guilt. So I just gathered all my swimming gear and got in the car where my mother was waiting. She didn't say much—no "well done" or "good job." But she smiled when I told her. That was her way of showing approval. She felt giving us too much praise would feed our ego and we wouldn't try harder the next time. And she always wanted us to keep trying harder, to get better and better results.

Somehow, this didn't discourage me. It raised the bar

of my own standards, of how I looked at things in life and what I expected of myself and others.

Yet still, I was rarely excited—those big feelings around my first achievement became quieter in later achievements and adventures. Whether it was a new place that I visited, a new experience in life, learning something new, or achieving something, I didn't feel excitement around it. It all felt like just a normal thing to go through, nothing to be excited about.

I don't think I even knew what excitement felt like. When I heard people say they were so excited they couldn't sleep, I had no idea how that felt. When my friends achieved something big and wanted to celebrate, I admired their sense of celebration but couldn't relate to it. And when I was praised by other people, I would feel very uncomfortable, even embarrassed, because I didn't think I had done well enough to deserve the praise. I was very critical of myself and the people around me, and constantly had high expectations of them and myself.

I did (and do) admire people who achieved great things, people like Steve Jobs, Mahatma Gandhi, Nelson Mandela, and Mother Teresa. Sometimes I also admired someone just delivering a great speech—as I listened to them, their words often touched my heart, and I wished

I could stand on the podium touching others, hearing the claps from the audience, and know I had made some difference.

Those I admired were persistent and hardworking, and had a dream they wanted to achieve in life. I wished I could have a dream like them, but I didn't know what it would be. Still, a little voice in my head told me that even though I didn't know what I wanted, I could do it if I put my heart into it.

I spent two years in Brunei, and the time served as a turning point in my young life. As I went from living in the metropolitan city of Hong Kong to living in quiet, simple, family-oriented Brunei, I experienced a stark contrast. It was a change that prepared me for future changes—the next being my first step into independence, as Mike, Barry, and I left our family home to attend school in the UK. It was a new world for us.

I still remember when we first arrived.

As I stepped out of the train with Mike and Barry, the sky was dark and it was quiet. We gathered our luggage and walked toward the exit of the small railway station. I could see the name of the town Tiverton written on the front—this was our destination—but there was no further guidance. There was no information booth, no attendant around, and very few other passengers who had gotten off with us. When we stepped out of the station, there was no taxi line, no bus station—just a small parking lot with a few cars parked inside.

My brothers and I looked at each other and wondered what we should do. While we were trying to figure it out, a middle-aged man who had also gotten off the train there approached us and asked where we wanted to go.

When Mike told him we wanted to go to East Devon College and asked where we could get a taxi, the man told us there wouldn't be any transportation that late, and the school was closed. He advised us to find a hotel to stay for a night.

We had no idea where to look for a hotel—it was 1976, and we didn't have Google Maps or a cell phone to use. The gentleman kindly offered us a lift to the local Chinese restaurant, thinking they might be able to help.

We drove for a few miles, on mostly country roads, until we reached a small street with some stores on both sides. They were closed except for the Chinese restaurant. We got out of the car with all our bags and thanked the gentleman for his kindness.

Mike went inside the restaurant while Barry and I stood on the pavement outside, guarding our belongings. After about twenty minutes, Mike came out of the restaurant with a young man, the owner's son, Ah Seng. We were so relieved to discover he spoke Cantonese and was from Hong Kong too. He took us to a nearby bed-and-breakfast where we stayed for a night, and the next day, he drove us to the school.

Ah Seng and his family's restaurant became our go-to place whenever we wanted a nice hot Chinese meal or needed information about local events.

We lived in the small town for four years as we attended college.

Tiverton is located in Devon, in the southwest part of England. East Devon College was small but international, with students from all parts of the world—Chinese students from Hong Kong, Malaysians, Indonesians, Iranians, Turks, Arabs, Europeans, Welsh, and the local English.

While we attended school, we lived in a basement we rented at Holly Lodge, a townhouse across from a small church. In front of the church was a graveyard, which we walked past every day. It didn't bother my brothers or me but some of our Asian friends would comment that the feng shui was not good. We lived too close to the dead people, they said; we would be haunted. I thought, though, that the church added some charm to the street.

Our place had a living room with sliding glass doors that extended to a small garden with bushes on both sides. There was also a small stream at the end of the garden where water would flow freely. You could feel nature right there in front of you. We had a small kitchen—it could only fit two people at one time—a front room with a single bed, another bedroom with two beds, and a bathroom. We had minimal furniture—a sofa with one armchair and a dining table with four chairs—but we found space for everyone who came over. John joined us from Brunei later that year, and eventually our place became the Asian headquarters of Tiverton, the go-to place for all new arrivals.

We started by having parties there during holidays and weekends, where we'd welcome anyone who wanted to join us. Gradually, our home became a popular gathering place for our Asian and English friends throughout the week too, especially during dinnertime. In a normal day, my brothers and I would cook for fifteen or more people at dinner—making fried rice, chicken wings with soy sauces, eggs with tomatoes, and fried vegetables Chinese style. We were used to having a big group of people at dinner back home so this made no difference for us.

We knew almost every Asian in the town of Tiverton.

Mike and me in front of Holly Lodge, Tiverton - UK, 1977

My circle of friends included not only other Asian students but also English students. They were my schoolmates and, at first, friends of friends. I was able to speak some mostly broken English because of my two years of school in Brunei, and I was determined to learn more. I came to hang out with my English-speaking friends most of the time, learning from them how to speak proper English. I also started to read simple English books to enhance my vocabulary. My brothers would watch Chinese VHS tapes and read mostly Chinese kung fu books, which gave them some kind of comfort being far away from home, but I, on the other hand, had different interests and intentions. I had come all the way to England to learn better English, so I wanted to spend my time doing just that.

On the second year in England, Mike started dating an English girl named Bev. She had fair skin and beautiful eyes–it was almost like they would transport you to a different place when you looked into them. She was also warm and friendly, with an infectious laugh, and we quickly became good friends. That year, we were invited by her parents, Bill and Pam, to have Christmas dinner with them.

I had never seen such a big turkey. We were offered the turkey breast, which was supposed to be the best part of the meat, along with vegetables, stuffing, and the pudding. All the dishes were new to us, and we were thankful for their kindness. The next year when we joined them for Christmas dinner again, I told Pam I would rather have the turkey legs or the wings, and they were surprised. The Chinese love their dark meat–it's usually more tender and tastier–but the turkey dark meat was hard to chew. It was different, and I learned that turkey is not the same as chicken.

These Christmas dinners became a tradition for us for the years to come.

Bill and Pam were lovely people, kind and generous. And because they took on exchange students every year, I met students from the US, Germany, and Asia who stayed with them. I had never known people who would open their house to other people to live with them before, and it felt very special. In Asia, most people have smaller homes, so you don't see or hear of people who do that, beyond maybe with their extended family. And even then, it is not for the whole school year. My experience with Bill and Pam stayed with me, and would encourage me to offer the same hospitality when I was older.

Communication in the late '70s was not as convenient as it is today—we were without computers, FaceTime, Zoom, or cell phones. We called our parents once every two months, standing in a public red phone booth with a few fifty-pence coins ready. The first fifty-pence coin let us reach an operator to connect the call—we had to talk very loudly because the reception was weak—then when the call went through and we heard the beep sound, we quickly put another fifty pence into the slot to avoid the line being cut off. My brothers and I took turns speaking to our parents. It was always quick, because otherwise it would cost too much for us.

My father visiting us in Twerton - UK, 1977.

During the summer breaks, we would go back to Brunei to see our parents. That was the only time in the year we saw them in person, and they were so happy to see us. They took us everywhere and whenever they saw their friends, they would say, "My kids just came back from England for the holiday." They were proud.

With my siblings and our parents, during summer holiday from school in England - Brunei, 1979

I began to work at my father's construction business over the summers, following his secretary, learning how to file documents, doing paperwork, recording business transactions, visiting clients with my dad, and joining site meetings with engineers. Dad's secretary gave me the simplest work, nothing very difficult or complicated, because she knew I was only there for a couple of months. But it formed the foundation of my understanding how business was conducted—at least what the process looked like. I really enjoyed learning it, especially as I always knew I would come back to help in the family business once I finished studying in England.

After four years at East Devon College, I completed my O and A levels and got accepted into a university in London, majoring in business administration. It was a sandwich course of four years that included one gap year.

The course wasn't my first choice—I had wanted to study law and become a lawyer—but Mike told me that if I studied law, I wouldn't be able to get married, that no man would want to marry a woman who was so strong. He knew I would want to become a barrister and felt it would be too intimidating to a man. Because I was naïve and because he was my older brother, I listened to him as I had for most of my life. I figured he must be right, and so I settled for my second choice studying business, which would help my family after graduation. I said goodbye to my brothers, who were all going to different universities in the country, and at the age of twenty-one, I began settling into a new city on my own.

London opened a new chapter of my life.

That first year there, I stayed with a Jewish lady, renting one bedroom on the second floor of her house. While there, I loved taking a long bath every night before bedtime, something that I learned in England. It was one of the things that I looked forward to every day. School was boring for me and it wasn't nearly as social an experience as at Tiverton; I made some friends, but we weren't very close. And of course I saw my brothers less, during holidays and long weekends. Yet I was content. I enjoyed the new freedom I felt.

In my second year in the course, I moved to a small flat of my own along the highway, with my own kitchen and small living room, one bedroom, and my own bathroom. It was the first time I lived by myself and it felt wonderful to me—I could do anything I wanted. I could leave the house anytime. Whether I cooked or didn't cook was entirely up to me. It felt so free not having to think or worry about my brothers or anyone else.

During my gap year, I got a nine-to-five job at a high street retail business, mostly doing commission-based sales. I learned fast and was good at selling.

One day, an African man walked in and wanted to buy a dress for his wife. When he asked if I could help him, I asked what size of dress he was looking for, and he said size eighteen. I knew the biggest size we had in the store was size fourteen. My brain started to work, thinking about how I might be able to help him and succeed in getting my commission too. In the shop, there were a few styles of dresses that came in a loose form or pleated without belts or waistline. I brought some pieces over to show him, stretching the dresses with my two hands wide open as far as I could reach, and putting them over my head to show him how they looked when they were on. He loved them and bought two pieces from me.

When he left the shop, he gave me one hundred pounds as a tip. I was speechless; a hundred pounds was like two weeks of my salary. The shop owner was very pleased with my performance, and told me that when I graduated, he would offer me a job as the shop manager if I decided to continue working for him. It never crossed my mind that I would get a job in London after I graduated— working for my dad in the family business was the only thing I had in mind.

After that summer was over, I began my final year in the course. Realizing what my studies were all about— preparing me for the future—I studied really hard that year. And then I graduated and was ready for my next stage.

After graduation I had planned to travel around Europe for at least one month. During my eight years in England, I had never been to any of its neighboring European countries, and I wanted to do that so I could really enjoy the full experience of being there before going back to Brunei.

But my dream of travelling to Europe vanished when a wedding was planned for that month.

Barry had met a lovely girl named Marie in England, who was Chinese, originally from Hong Kong, but had grown up in England. They had been dating for a few years and were very much in love, and he wanted to get married right after his graduation and take her back to Brunei.

I knew he didn't want to lose her because it might be hard for them to maintain a long-distance relationship. I know Mike also advised Barry to propose to her soon, saying if he didn't, he would lose her. Barry took his advice like I had and brought my mother to London to meet Marie's parents. Once the parents had met, the wedding was underway.

It would be held back home, the first wedding in my family, and my father invited almost everyone he knew there. Brunei is such a small country that with news like this, everyone would know. So if you didn't invite certain people, that would be remembered for a long time. My father was considered a reputable businessman and knew a lot of people, so it was important to keep the peace. That made it a big occasion—there were no restaurants big enough to accommodate all the guests we wanted to invite, and we decided to rent a school hall as the wedding venue.

My father wanted me to make a speech on his behalf to all the distinguished guests, most of them government officials and businessmen. He insisted that I return to Brunei for the wedding; after all, it was the first wedding in the family. I was not very happy but I also didn't want to miss my brother's big day. Dad tried to comfort me, saying, "You can always go back after the wedding."

My brother Barry's wedding, in front of our house. My grandpa, two of my grandmas, and my great-grandma were among those sitting in the front - Brunei, 1985

And he was right—after the wedding, I could have gone back to England or travelled to somewhere else in Europe, but it was such a long journey from Brunei that instead I just jumped right into the business. It was the normal thing to do for most children when they completed school, especially if they were a part of a family business.

I followed my father to all his business meetings, learned how to do a tender for roadwork and construction projects, had lunch with bankers to discuss loans or negotiate a better interest rate for the projects, learned how to open a letter of credit to purchase machinery, worked with subcontractors and engineers to understand the progress of the project, and submitted invoices to the government after certain parts of a project were completed. I would also go to see the minister of the public works department with my dad to give progress reports on our projects, so the payment would release to fund the rest of the work. After a few times, Dad just sent me there by myself, after having coached me on what to say, what to ask for, and how to talk to the minister. Those were great experiences for me, and how my dad trained me in the business. Some of these projects were sizable enough we couldn't handle them ourselves, and so we invited other overseas construction companies to do a joint venture. Because we were a Brunei-registered company, we were the main contractor; although the overseas companies were much bigger than we were, they still needed to come in under our company as a subcontractor. In this way, we worked with construction firms from Korea, Japan, the US, and the Philippines that were ten or more times bigger than us.

My first project was the Brunei Sultan Palace. It was huge, with 1,800 rooms. It had a mosque and rooms for the Gurkha—UK soldiers there to protect the sultan from any invasion by neighboring countries. (Brunei is a former British colony. It gained its independence from the United Kingdom on January 1, 1984.)

The palace was built after the country gained its independence, to house the sultan's wife, his many children, servants, and security teams. The interior design was glamorous—it was where the sultan received foreign diplomats and guests, and hosted New Year parties and other official events. It was magnificent. I had never seen anything built at such a scale.

My father's company was responsible for the supply of stones and aggregates used for the palace and some smaller buildings too. The designer for the project was a Philippine company called Ayala, and the management company was Batel Construction Corporation, from the United States. And then there I was, wearing a construction helmet and holding a folder full of the minutes of a project meeting, the schedule and projected timeline, etc.

I walked into a room with my father's chief engineer, John, and fifteen others, including other engineers, project managers, the site foreman, and other top management people. Although I didn't know all of the details of the project, I felt good to be part of such an important group, and I listened closely to all they said.

It was a feeling that I couldn't quite define, but it excited me. I felt a deep confidence. Although the group was much older and definitely more experienced than I was, I didn't feel intimidated.

Experiences like these opened up my worldview, and my confidence grew because of that. I have never felt uncomfortable or scared by any situation in business. It always felt like a natural thing to me, even at age seven when I would sit at the breakfast table with my dad and his clients. Working in the business, I wasn't even afraid to call up a managing director to demand payment. I remember one time when a construction company had owed us money for more than 120 days, which was very overdue considering our normal sixty-day payment schedule. I picked up the phone, called the managing director, and asked for payment, explaining that we needed the money for the second phase of the project. He politely laughed and asked me if I understood the relationship between him and my father. I too replied politely, saying that I was sure they were very good friends but I also told him it was business—there was nothing personal about my request. He made the payment soon after the call, and eventually, we became good friends too.

I was able to separate our business from the personal and not get too emotionally involved in the decision that I made. I supposed he admired me for that courage. My grandfather used to tell me, "Business is about making money. If you don't want to make money, you should not go into business. But in business you should also remember, let other people make money too—if they don't, it will not be a long-term business for us."

These words taught me that we shouldn't be afraid to ask for what we deserve, but we also need to be fair to others and not expect to make all the money in the world. We need to let others make theirs too.

This has been a guiding principle for how I do business in my life, always trying my best to be fair. These experiences in Brunei were the beginning of this, and paved the road for my future.

One sunny day in the late summer of 1985, I was sitting at a local restaurant with a friend visiting from Singapore. We were enjoying the spicy curry fish head and beef satay, chatting about our work and our lives, when he told me about a huge earthquake in Mexico that had killed and injured many people. I asked when it had happened, and he told me it had happened almost a week ago. I was surprised I hadn't read or hear anything about it.

I read about it in the local newspaper two days later, and was astonished and disturbed by the fact that it had taken more than a week to appear in our local news.

"Where am I?" I asked myself.

I felt a sense of fear come to me, as if I was on some remote island, not knowing what was going on with the rest of the world. I felt disconnected and terrified. It bothered me so much that I decided to do something about it. (It might sound as if I was overreacting, but I literally felt like I was trapped on an island.)

I had no idea what I would do or where I would live; I just wanted to get out.

I went home that night and had dinner with my siblings and parents like I did most nights. Then after dinner was over, I went into the living room where my father sat watching TV. I sat next to him and told him that I wanted to go back to Hong Kong.

My father was quiet. He didn't ask me why, almost as if he had already known I wouldn't stay long in Brunei or perhaps felt I was a rebellious type who would certainly want my freedom. Instead, he just asked, "What are you going to do in Hong Kong?"

I quickly told him that I would look for a job, I just had no clue what it would be. I said I wanted to work for others to gain more experience, which was true. Almost all my experience in life until then was with the family business. Everyone in the company knew I was the boss's daughter—so they would listen to me, no questions asked, even when I made mistakes. And when I did make mistakes, they would help me correct them. I wanted to prove to myself I had what it took to be in a senior management position with a big firm and not my own family business where I was sheltered by my parents. Father didn't reply. He walked into the bedroom with my mom and they didn't come out for an hour.

It felt like an eternity to me as I sat in my own room with my nerves, wondering what the next step would be if my parents wouldn't let me go.

I was determined to leave Brunei. And I wanted to see the world.

Hong Kong had come to mind because it was the only place I felt comfortable going to at that time. It was my birthplace, it was a metropolitan city of the world, and even though I hadn't returned since I left at the age of thirteen, it still felt better than staying in Brunei. I also thought of England. I had been there for eight years, I knew London well, and I had friends there too. But I felt it might be too far away from my family.

These are the only two places I had lived so far other than Brunei, and I didn't want to think too much about any other places. I just wanted to get out first.

When my father came into my room, I was lying on my bed. He sat down on the chair next to me and I quickly stood up, not knowing what to expect. He looked at me and said in a calm voice, "I will give you two choices. One is to stay in Brunei to continue working for the family business. The second is to go back to Hong Kong to start another family business."

I was so excited that I almost jumped up and screamed. This was the second time in my life that I had felt such excitement, the first having been my completion of my swimming gold medal. I was smiling as I told my dad I would go back to Hong Kong to start a new business.

My heart was full of joy and excitement, ready to explode. It was such a relief, knowing I had an opportunity to do something different in a different country. I had loved living in Brunei, being with my family, and being at my job there too, but somehow it hadn't been enough for me—even before I learned of the earthquake. I had wanted more, without knowing what it was. I knew there was more to offer out there and I was hungry for it.

The earthquake was a trigger that surfaced the depth of my desire to want more, to grow, to see the world. And now I would. Although I would still be working for my family, my ultimate goal was to leave Brunei and this change would let me do so. And the unknown that was ahead of me seemed to stir up my excitement and give me energy and hope.

That night, I packed two suitcases and bought a ticket to Hong Kong. I left Brunei the very next day.

Chapter 3

A MARRIAGE OF TWO FAMILIES

W hen my father told me to set up another family business in Hong Kong, he didn't say what kind of business I should do. I don't think he knew; he wanted me to find my own direction, much like he did when he first went to Brunei. He was an entrepreneur, as was his father, and it was time for me to become one too.

The money needed would be provided by my father—I was not to worry about that. Like in many Asian family businesses, my parents provided the resources for the children, we kids worked for the family, and we got our salary from the family too. It was a big help knowing I could do anything I wanted in this new venture and have the financial support I needed.

I began by finding a space to work from.

I met a real estate agent in the Kowloon area of Hong Kong on a hot summer day when it was humid and the sun was particularly strong. As I walked down the busy street, I noticed the noise of cars and buses and the rush of people all around me. Trucks were loading off goods onto the sidewalk, and people were everywhere, coming in and out of office buildings, hurrying along busy with their lives, talking loudly, dressed professionally. Men wore suits and ties, and women wore fashionable dresses with a jacket, high heels, and pantyhose.

It was such a contrast to life in Brunei.

In Hong Kong, the energy was infectious. I was excited just by observing everything I could see and hear. I felt alive.

When the man from the real estate agency arrived to meet me, I saw he too was well dressed in a suit and tie, carrying a folder with descriptions of the office units he was about to show me. We took the lift to the ninth floor, where we got out and walked into a big, empty space with concrete walls and floors. It was spacious, with windows that stretched from one side of the wall to the next. Looking out the windows, I could see the street below was full of people, full of life. I already felt in love with the place.

The agent began explaining how many rooms I could partition and how many desks I could have in this space. He also told me about the location and the other tenants. I was listening and learning, pretending I knew everything he said but much was unfamiliar. I was a fast learner, though, and two months later I moved into the office, renovated it, hired a secretary, and set it up with desks, fax machines, telephone lines, and desktop computers. The company was registered and ready to do business. Brunei already seemed like history to me.

While I was trying to figure out what kind of business we should do, I began acting like a buying office for our Brunei company, purchasing used machinery and spare parts from other countries. Whatever spare parts our company couldn't find locally, I would source globally and charge a fee as a commission. It helped pay for our employees' salary and my own living. I still needed to find other ways to build the business, though, and later that year, I found one when I had an opportunity to become a distribution agent for a handheld, portable fax machine.

I thought it was such an innovation. The machine was like a small typewriter and weighed around twenty pounds. It could transmit a fax from anywhere, saving so much time; I was fascinated by the technology and thought it was a great business. I even got featured in a local newspaper, explaining the function of the machine. I hired four salespeople, who brought the machines around to other offices every day to demonstrate their function. Our office was busy all the time, yet despite our good intentions and excitement, the business didn't do well. We lost money and closed the business after a year. The technology world was moving too fast, and no one wanted to carry a twenty-pound machine around the busy streets of Hong Kong with a suit on.

This gave me my first taste of an unsuccessful business venture; I was twenty-five years old. I didn't feel good about the money lost, but that didn't stop me from looking for something else to do. Around that time, Mike decided to join me in Hong Kong, and we discussed working together. I was closest with him among my brothers and we worked well together—although we had disagreements, we always worked things out. We agreed on an idea, and then I began most of its execution.

It was 1986, and Hong Kong was still a British colony, operating under British law. It would be more than ten years before it returned to China, but even then, I knew that China would become a superpower in the future and so that was the market we needed to tap into. Mike and I decided to start making trips to mainland China, and through our contacts in business, we met up with people there who were eager to help and pave the road for us in exchange for a small fee.

Everything was new to China, which gave us great business possibility. We began doing trading through our Hong Kong office in a range of areas, from buying goat hairs for a Korean cosmetic brush company to selling coat hangers for motels in Texas. We also imported carpet from the US and eventually owned a carpet mill in Georgia; after a couple of years, we bought the whole carpet plant along with its machinery and sent it all to China to open the country's first integrated carpet plant in a joint venture with a local Chinese company. We would try anything, things that we had never done before. It was exciting, new, and adventurous. I was never afraid to go into a different business, even if it was new to me—I would hire people with knowledge in the industry to join us, and I would learn from them. Even being my own boss at a young age, I knew I needed to be humble around things that I didn't know, and I learned how to listen and be fair to others. All that I had learned from my grandfather and father then came into play. I was lucky to also have good people who worked for us. By then, we had managers, salespeople, an accountant, supporting staff, and secretaries.

A year or so later, Barry's family—which now included a beautiful daughter I love named Jeannie—and my younger brother John also joined us in Hong Kong. My parents had bought a big house in the prestigious part of Kowloon, and my mother and grandma moved back to live with us. My father commuted between Brunei and Hong Kong.

Mike got married later that year to a nice Korean girl, Ceci, followed by John, who married a Japanese girl, Hiroko, he met while finishing his studies there. We were back to one big family, except this time, it was our own international family.

When I was twenty-six years old, I walked into a cocktail party in Taiwan. I was about to meet my ex-husband.

I was wearing a black tuxedo suit, satin jacket lapels, a white dress shirt with cuff links underneath, and three-inch heels. I felt confident. I knew I looked good. The cocktail party was to celebrate a joint venture between a Taiwanese conglomerate and US-based Purina to open a chicken feed meal plant in Taichung. It was my first time visiting Taiwan and my Chinese Mandarin wasn't fluent—I could follow most of the conversation thanks to my six years of Chinese education in Hong Kong, but to communicate in the language was a different matter.

I was with my grandfather's business friend, an older Taiwanese woman whom I didn't like very much. She kept telling my mother that I was working too hard in Hong Kong, not dating anyone, that soon I would be over marrying age and it would be hard to find a man to marry. Marriage wasn't something I was thinking about then—I told myself I wouldn't want to get married until at least age thirty, which might be considered late for a Chinese girl of my generation, but I didn't care. I was enjoying my freedom and most of all, I was enjoying my business career.

This woman had tried some matchmaking while I was in Taiwan, and did introduce me to a man from a nice family, but her attempts didn't work.

While we stood together at the cocktail party, a man approached us. "Are you sisters?" he asked.

I thought it was a strange question. The woman I was with was old enough to be my mom. The question didn't leave much of an impression on me and our exchange with the man was short. I was also introduced to an elderly couple, Don and Janie from America, with whom I felt a strong connection. The next day, I met them for breakfast at their hotel and it turned out they had been the host family for the man I met the night before, when he was studying in the US. His name was Gary.

The breakfast was the beginning of a close friendship with Don and Janie, who would eventually become like American parents to me.

Janie and me at Janie and Don's home - Virginia, US, 1992

Don and me at the nursing home where he lived in his final years - Florida , US, 2010

They knew Gary's family well because they had hosted him during his American studies. Gary was born the youngest of three in Taiwan, where males have a civic duty to do a two-year compulsory military service when they reach the age of eighteen. Because of this, his parents sent him to study in Singapore for high school at the age of thirteen, then to America for college, in a spirit of love and protection, to avoid the military service. It wasn't uncommon for those who could afford to do it. Gary arrived in the US speaking little English, much like me when I was in England, but he was a smart guy, studied well, and graduated from a prestigious school in Washington, DC. He worked for a few years in the States, mainly doing investments for his family, then returned to Taiwan to help in his father's business. Shortly after he returned, I met him at the party, which I had discovered was hosted by his father.

I stayed for a few more days in Taiwan, travelling around and visiting some beautiful places. When it was time to go back to Hong Kong, I called Gary's father to thank him for inviting us to the party. As I spoke with him, he was kind enough to invite me to lunch before I left.

We met at a posh Chinese restaurant in a private room beautifully decorated with Chinese antiques and paintings. The food was delicious and the service was attentive. The waitress was standing behind us, pouring tea, handing out the napkins, and serving us the food, when Gary suddenly walked in. I hadn't expected to meet him again. Our conversation was polite, with him asking where I went to school, what business I did in Hong Kong, and that sort of thing. After lunch, we said goodbye, and Gary's father had his driver take me to the airport. I returned to Hong Kong.

A few weeks later, I received a call from Gary. I was surprised. Even more so when he said he wanted to visit me in Hong Kong to talk about a business opportunity.

When he arrived, I picked him up from the airport and began showing him around Hong Kong. We went to the beaches on the south side, visited the temples, and ate some of the local foods Hong Kong was famous for. He asked me how often I visited China and what it was like to do business there. It was casual conversation, simple curiosity, I thought. But we began to see each other more often and over the following months we started dating. I went to Taiwan to see him, and he came to Hong Kong to see me, mostly on weekends. We had a good time together, and he was very much a gentleman, opening doors for me and serving me food when we ate out.

Our feelings for each other grew and then one day he asked me, "Have you been to America?" I said no, and he immediately offered to take me there. I didn't want to go with him alone, so I invited Barry and his wife, Marie, to join us. This worked out well, since Barry was the same age as Gary, and Marie and I had a good relationship ever since our time in England together.

Two weeks later, we all arrived in New York. This was the first time that I had set foot in America, and as I stood on the famous Fifth Avenue, I couldn't believe my eyes. Everything was so huge—tall buildings, shops everywhere, lasting for miles. I thought London was big compared to

Hong Kong, but New York was like a different world to me. I had never seen such a massive city.

We visited the Empire State Building, the World Trade Center, and Central Park. We crossed the Brooklyn Bridge, and we explored the streets. It was so new to me, so full of excitement. After New York City, we travelled to Washington, DC, where Don and Janie lived. After spending two nights there, we travelled to San Francisco where I visited some of my family friends from Brunei, and then we flew to Hawaii.

After we checked in to the hotel in Hawaii, we walked around Waikiki Beach. The air was clean and everything felt so spacious. I felt a sense of freedom in this big country. I didn't know why exactly, but somehow, it captivated me.

After dinner, we returned to our room and Gary suddenly asked me, "Why don't we get married?" It was a shock to me, and it took me awhile to respond. We had been dating for less than four months.

I didn't say yes or no—I just replied, "Don't you think it's a bit too soon?"

It was certainly not what I expected from him, but I did like him. He was very nice and attentive to my needs, and very much a gentleman—he opened doors for me, he would pay for meals without hesitation, he would even offer to pay for my shopping if I let him. As a husband, I knew he would let me do anything I wanted to do.

I liked him because he was respectful but I didn't have butterflies in my stomach. I didn't know how I was supposed to feel when I was in love—I did miss him when we weren't together, but that was it. I clearly wasn't head over heels for him, but everything else seemed quite compatible. Our family backgrounds were very similar, which felt important to me then. We both worked for our family business. He was western educated, which meant he had lived outside his home country and would understand different cultures and hopefully see things with an open mind. And he had good manners and was a gentleman. These were the things I thought were the essential criteria in any marriage. And so when he proposed, I hesitated to say yes but I also didn't want to say no. We just left it there, and the next day we returned to Hong Kong. As time passed and we continued to see each other, at some point we eventually knew we would get married.

The following few months when I went to Taiwan, I also spent a lot of time with Gary's father, going with him and Gary to meetings where he was the chairman or on the committee. The traditional Chinese way of doing business was quite new to me, but building relationships was something I had learned from my father at a young age. Gary's father was doing the same. He was always busy with his work, but he always found time for me and his son when I was in town. Gary's mother, on the other hand, was a very private and quiet person, and I didn't get to meet her until it was time to set a date for the wedding.

When we met, she was distant but offered a friendly smile. She didn't ask anything about me or my family, as if she had already known everything, and perhaps she did. Our conversation was courteous and short, and I felt she wasn't very keen to get to know me. But Gary was her baby. She loved him the most among all her three children, and treated him like a little boy even though he was almost thirty years of age at that time.

I had a strange feeling about a grown man being so pampered by his mother—it crossed my mind that Gary might be very protected by his parents—but I didn't put too much thought into it.

Gary's brother was also planning his wedding that year and because he was older, he got to marry first, so we had to wait for a year. It was the Chinese custom, which I had never before known.

Gary's parents came to meet my parents at our new home in Stanley, a coastal town in the southern part of

Hong Kong. There weren't many places like Stanley; it was a beautiful area, and my parents' house faced the Stanley beach, where you could see the ocean, listen to the sound of the sea, and feel the open air. The conversation of our parents was polite, somewhat formal but pleasant.

Gary's father was very much interested in China, particularly the political situation, and because my dad had many experiences there, they were deep in conversation around the topic. The conversation between my mother and Gary's mom was light. That night, we booked a private room at a Chinese restaurant for dinner, and over the next few days, I took Gary's parents around Hong Kong to do shopping, sightseeing, and eating before they returned to Taiwan. After all of our parents met, the next thing was to pick a good date for the wedding. The date was set for twelve months later.

I didn't need to get involved in the details of the wedding except for my dress. Gary's father and two of his secretaries took charge of the event. I had no clue who was invited, who would be there, what the wedding would look like, or where it would be held. I wasn't consulted about the menu, guest lists, flowers, or what kind of cake I would like. I was just told to invite my parents and brothers from Hong Kong. Everything else was taken care of by someone else.

I thought it was a normal Taiwanese wedding at the time, but later I realized it was a wedding that showed off the status of Gary's family, in particular his father. There were over two thousand people who attended in Taiwan.

But first, six months before we would marry in Taiwan, we had a ceremony in the US. Gary was a US citizen and his father, as a businessman, Taiwan senator, and chairman of the National Federation of Industries of the Republic of China thought it would be a good idea for us to have a wedding there. He was planning a trip to the US for a corn purchase, and he wanted to invite all the committee members who would be travelling with him, as well as the US Secretary of Agriculture and agriculture committee members. He was using the wedding as part of his business relationship building, across continents. Our friend Don was working for the US government at that time, and he helped organize the event.

The night before the wedding, I had a big argument with Gary. Right in the middle of the night, he woke me up, angry, telling me that we couldn't be more different, that we didn't have much in common, and questioning why we were together. I was shocked beyond belief. What was he talking about? Who was this person? There was no sign of this coming; he had been good to me in every way until that moment—kind, attentive, and a gentleman all the times we were together. Now when we were just a few hours away from becoming husband and wife, he was questioning our marriage.

I didn't know what to say. I was crying, angry, and in disbelief. I kept asking him what he meant; did he know we were going to get married the next day? He was pacing the room, talking angrily, and said things that were hurtful.

After about half an hour, which felt like an eternity for me, I couldn't stay with him anymore. I grabbed my jacket and ran down to the hotel lobby. There was no one in the lobby that late, and I was alone. Everything blurred in front of my eyes. Tears were streaming down my face and I couldn't see anything. I was scared and confused—I couldn't believe this was happening to me. I had no one to go to.

I sat on a chair in the corner, looking out the window and at the trees outside. It was quiet. I wanted to run away but I was in a foreign place and I was scared. Where could I go?

My brain struggled to make sense out of this. Don would soon be arriving to pick us up and go to the church. I kept asking myself, What should I do? How could I go along with the wedding?

But then I would think of the people who would be coming to the church—if we didn't get married, what would that do to his father's reputation if I walked away from it? He would be so embarrassed and angry. What would others think of him? What would the newspaper write about it? It would be a laughingstock in Taiwan, and I couldn't do that to him.

Yet, what about my own happiness? Did I want to marry someone who didn't love me at all?

I was confused but my mind kept returning to what this would do to his father.

As I was struggling to find the right answer to the solution, Gary came into the lobby and walked over to me. He apologized for his behavior earlier on, said he had a nightmare and that he didn't know what he was talking about, and told me he was sorry. He held my hand and asked me to return to the room.

I was motionless, staring off into space. I didn't say anything but my body slowly stood up and walked back to the room.

The next thing I knew I was putting on makeup to try to cover my swollen eyes and taking out my dress to put it on.

Janie was waiting for me in the lobby to take me to the hair salon, and after that we would go to the church.

I pretended nothing had happened; my brain tried to block off the night before. But everything was unreal. The ceremony, the people who came to wish us happiness, the cocktail party—all seemed like a dream to me. I didn't know why I was going through with the whole thing. I was doing it just to save face for someone else. What was I thinking?

Years later, when I told Don about the incident, he asked me why I didn't walk away from it. Why would I put other people above my own happiness?

I didn't know then, but I know now. I was taught at a very young age that respecting others, especially the elderly, is an important virtue to have. We were not taught to ask ourselves what we wanted because it was considered selfish. We were supposed to always anticipate what others in the family needed and I had always done so—like when I stood up at the dinner table to get ready to fetch rice for my grandfather, like when I didn't pursue my law degree because my brother told me I shouldn't. I had listened to the family and did what I was told. Family harmony was important. We didn't want argument. We should keep our unhappiness to ourselves, because family comes first. And family would always take care of us. These were deeply ingrained in my mind.

I couldn't bring myself to walk away from the wedding because of how it would affect others. It was okay for me to not get what I wanted, but I couldn't shame my or Gary's family.

The ceremony was small and held in a church in Fairfax County in Northern Virginia. I stood there in a simple white dress with no veil with Gary in a suit and tie, as the pastor conducted our ceremony in a Christian way in front of about fifty guests. My parents weren't there—it was too far for them to come, and anyway, we would be having a second wedding celebration in Asia. Don walked me down the aisle.

Most of the people there were Taiwan joint-working committee members, with a few newspaper reporters among them who would report what the committee had achieved on the trip back to Taiwan. After the church service, we had a cocktail party in a DC hotel, where I met with politicians, government officials mostly from the agriculture department, senators, congressmen, and businesspeople from the US. This was the first time I had met with politicians in America. Some of them became lifelong friends.

After the ceremony, we went back to Taiwan, and it was almost like the incident the night before the wedding never happened. Gary was kind to me, still opened my doors, and would give me anything I asked for. We never mentioned that night, but still, the feeling between us was different. We were a couple but without a sense of intimacy—behind closed doors, we were just friends. We didn't argue much, and we generally did our own things, except on the business side. We still lived separately, with the plan to move in together after our wedding in Taiwan.

The wedding was held at the top-floor ballroom of the Grand Hotel in Taipei, an elegant hotel that had hosted many foreign dignitaries. The entrance of our wedding hall was decorated with flowers, lots of them. Two of our wedding photos blown up like giant posters were placed in front of the hall so that the guests would recognize us, the bride and groom. Inside the gigantic hall was a stage, with a flower-lined path leading to it. There were beautiful ladies dressed in cheongsam to greet the guests.

When the wedding started, there was a signing ceremony with both witnesses of the bride and groom. They were supposed to be people who knew us well, but I had no idea who they were. Gary and I stood in the middle of the stage for a long time. When we were announced husband and wife, a big ball fell down from the celling just above our heads and broke open with thousands of little pieces of shiny paper, much like you see on *American Idol*. It was like a movie for me, so unreal. We spent five hours standing with smiles on our faces pretending to be excited and happy, greeting people who came over to wish us well. None of these well-wishers were people that I knew, and I was quite sure the same was true for Gary.

The next day, I moved into his parents' home, where we planned to live for a few months until our own apartment would be ready. That same night, he disappeared and was gone for three days without a word. Even his parents didn't know where he was.

I couldn't believe he would leave me alone with his parents at their home. What kind of man would do that to his newlywed wife? I was so angry that I moved out of their place and checked into a hotel.

A day later, his mother showed up at the door of my hotel room, begging for me to come home. She told me she didn't do a good job of raising her son and this had caused me to suffer.

This became a pattern of our life. Whenever we had an argument, his parents would come to see me and apologize to me for what they didn't do. His mother would come or his father would come, telling me Gary was wrong, that he should not have treated me this way or that way, but in the end, nothing changed. Gary did what he wanted.

I split my time between China, Taiwan, Hong Kong, and the US—work became my escape that kept me from looking deep down into my own feelings. For the next few years, I put all my time and energy into it.

It was a sensitive time between China and Taiwan. The first time Gary went to China, he was so nervous when the plane landed and he saw soldiers carrying guns patrolling the airport. He asked me if it was safe to go. He was worried he would be questioned by the Communist Party about his intention to enter the country because of his Taiwanese status. By that time, I had already been travelling quite frequently between Hong Kong and China, so I told him there was nothing to worry about.

In the early '90s, Gary's father led a business delegation to China, which Gary and I joined, and we were well received by the Chinese government. Even the Chinese premier came to greet us. While we were in Beijing, the capital of China, Gary's father went to meet with the president of China. This trip was big news in Taiwan because it was the first delegation of its kind travelling to the mainland. By then, we had opened up our first plant in

China, which was considered one of the early Taiwanese investments into China. It was an important step for Gary's family business and certainly a proud moment for his father.

China became a place where we regularly visited, and by the mid-1990s, we completed building four plants there. I did a lot of the liaison work between the Chinese companies and Gary's company, while at the same time overseeing the business in my own family.

I travelled constantly during the first few years of our marriage and my knowledge of business expanded in every city and country I travelled to. There were always new things to learn. Back home in Taiwan, I also accompanied Gary and his father to all kinds of business events, meeting different businessmen and government officials. Gary's father was proud to take me with him. We travelled together, we ate together, we talked about business together.

Gary's father was a self-made businessman who lost his parents at a very young age. Because he was the oldest, he took up the job of looking after his three siblings. He put them in an orphanage while he worked to bring in money for their food and education, and eventually he took them back out.

He once told me that it was his dream to own a business so he could wear his white shirt, suit, and tie every day, and he did. He had a very high standard, including the way he dressed. I was the only one he would trust to go shopping with and he would ask for my advice, even with his home renovation. I would pick up the fabric for his suit or choose shoes for him. Gary was pleased because it felt good for him to know his wife was well liked by his father—this was the most important part of his life, pleasing his father.

I enjoyed my relationship with his father. We respected and appreciated each other. I could handle the business, have good conversations when I joined business meetings, speak good English, and translate for his father as needed. I was well dressed and never disappointed him; I seldom said no to anything asked of me. I was on autopilot, thinking this was what life was all about. And I have to admit, I enjoyed the experience and got to learn a lot from him, especially in business. He was a fighter—whatever problems he had in his life, he would solve them and I admired him for that.

I was so busy in my work life that I rarely thought about whether I was happy or not in my marriage. I got to travel first class, stay at the best hotels, meet new people, enjoy the challenge of new business, and I had money to spend. What wasn't there to like about this? I got to see my parents and family whenever I wanted; flying from Hong Kong to Taiwan was only one and a half hours by plane. Everything seemed normal to me. My mother, my sisters-in-law, and my nieces and nephew often came to visit me in Taiwan, where we would travel around the island, eat out in nice restaurants, and go shopping. I never felt lonely because I got to see them so much.

But while I didn't feel lonely, I was certainly alone in my marriage.

Chapter 4

THE DENIAL

As time passed, I felt more and more lonely.

Most nights, Gary took me to dinner and then dropped me off back home, saying he had business meetings to attend. I would watch TV—which was valuable in helping me learn to speak and write Mandarin—and then have a long hot bath before turning the lights off. By the time Gary returned home it was usually past 3 a.m. Sometimes he would come home drunk, needing a friend to carry him into our house. His friend and I would put him in bed, and it would be a lucky night if he didn't throw up. I always had a trash bin next to the bed just in case.

The next day, his father would call to look for him and wasn't happy when he found out he was still sleeping. I would tell Gary when he woke up that his father called, and Gary would be angry at me for not lying.

I refused to lie for him. "You can tell him yourself," I would say.

I had many serious conversations with him over the years of our marriage. I told him it wasn't fair to me. "Don't push me into the corner, I don't know what I would do," I would say, threatening that I might leave him if he carried on behaving this way. One time, he negotiated with me. "I will stay home three nights a week, and the rest of the time I can do what I want." I thought about this. Knowing it was difficult for anyone to make changes overnight, I thought perhaps if I gave him some time to work on it, he might slowly change. I was still trying to be nice. I said, "Okay, let's give it a try." This didn't last for a week.

I was not sure he was having an affair with another woman, but I didn't want to think too much about it. I kept telling myself that he was young, he still wanted to hang out with his friends, singing karaoke and having fun. He wasn't violent, and when we were together, he was still nice to me. He still put food on my plate when we ate together, which I actually hated but knew he meant it kindly. When he was sober, he was like a normal person, even a gentleman. We still travelled for business together, attending meetings with his father. He never raised his voice to me or did anything harmful. We still never referred to that conversation the night before our wedding, but once he did tell me that he didn't like to be in Taiwan, that he would rather go back to the US. I asked him why he felt this way, but he never gave me an answer.

As time went on, I spent more and more time with my parents and I got so used to it that eventually I didn't miss having him around at night. Gradually it became normal to me too. I cared for him but I didn't love him. To be honest, I didn't even know what love was.

Once, I told my mother Gary couldn't get up in the morning because he came home late at night. She made an excuse for him that he might be working hard, so let him sleep.

I knew that wasn't the case, but I didn't argue with her. And that was the last time I brought up my marriage problems with her. Many years later, she told me that she had also been suffering in her own marriage with my father. My father had many affairs during their marriage—it was a normal thing for a man to stray, especially businessmen. Women, on the other hand, were just like machines to have children and raise them on their own.

I didn't see my father much when I was young. He was always travelling and busy with his work.

I asked her, "Why didn't you leave him?" She kept saying she couldn't leave us; she saw no future for herself. Instead of fighting it, she might as well accept it as her destiny. Divorce in her generation was almost unheard of. No one wanted to marry someone who had been through divorce, let alone with four children.

My father was a good father to us. He worked hard to provide for the family and he loved my brothers and me very much. He never raised his voice to us, even if we made mistakes—he would complain to my mother or even scold her for not doing her job well but he never did the same to us. But he was not a good husband.

My mother never put her own happiness at the forefront; it was always the family first. She believed as a Chinese woman, her family was her soul, even if it was broken. She needed to protect it, especially her children.

Now I understand why she defended Gary when I was complaining. She knew he was not right but she didn't want me to feel hurt like she did. She definitely didn't want me to think he might be having an affair with another woman. Instead she wanted me to think differently, even if it was a lie, her way to protect me from getting hurt.

After three years of marriage, I finally got pregnant.

I was so happy. I was going to be a mother, and it was such a wonderful feeling. I was overjoyed. Knowing I would have a child, my own child, was beyond what I could describe in words.

Some part of me also hoped that with a child, a family, Gary's behavior might change. I hoped he would become more mature, more responsible, and more settled. When I told him the news, he was happy, and even happier when he found out it was a boy! He knew his father would be very happy.

While I was pregnant, I kept travelling as usual between Hong Kong and Taiwan, spending more and more time in Hong Kong working on both family businesses. I continued to enjoy my freedom to do what I wanted in my business life, and I enjoyed being with my family in Hong Kong, staying for weeks at a time. I had so much variety in my life. With the baby on the way, I found my own happiness, something to look forward to, and it was a wonderful feeling. Not having Gary around didn't bother me anymore. And I was sure he was happy he didn't have to worry about me being alone at home.

I had decided to have the baby in Hong Kong to be closer to my mom, so she could help me after the baby was born.

Three weeks from my due date, I was staying at an apartment not too far from my parents' home in Kowloon, with a live-in helper named Rose, a Filipino woman who helped look after me at that time. It was the Chinese New Year's Eve in 1989. After I finished our family New Year's Eve dinner, my younger brother John drove Rose and me home.

It was a quiet and calm night in the street, since most of the people at that hour were celebrating New Year's Eve with their family. It was a change from the usual busy and bustling city.

When we arrived at my apartment, John dropped us off and went to park his car. He would then come up to check on us. Rose and I got into the lift, and we headed up to the eleventh floor. Suddenly, the lift stopped. The light went off and it was pitch dark. We couldn't see anything and didn't even know which floor we were on. Rose was very nervous; she was afraid I would give birth to the baby inside the lift. I, on the other hand, felt quite calm. I kept comforting her by saying that someone would come to our rescue soon.

When John made his way into the building, he realized that we had gotten stuck inside the lift. He ran from floor to floor to find us. I could hear him calling my name and asking me where I was, but the noise was far away; I knew he was on the wrong floor. Finally, he located us on the floor where we had gotten trapped. He kept yelling, "Don't panic, I will go find help!"

It was Chinese New Year's Eve, and no one was working at that hour, including the lift engineer.

I sat on the floor inside the lift, holding my big tummy while comforting Rose so she wouldn't worry, telling her that help was on the way. It was almost two hours later when I saw a small crack of light coming through the lift door. It was the engineer. He got us out but couldn't fix the lift that night. It didn't bother me; we walked up the two flights of steps and went into my apartment. John went back to his house; I took a bath and retired to sleep.

In the middle of the night, my water broke.

I called my doctor who told me to quickly pack a few clothes and head to the hospital immediately. I called my brother John to come pick me up, and he walked up eleven flights of stairs to my apartment and walked down eleven flights of stairs with me to his car. Then we rushed to the hospital. I called my mother, who left to meet us too.

My son, Albert, was born after eleven hours of labor that night, on Chinese New Year Day. That year, according to the Chinese zodiac, was the Year of the Snake.

The next day, my father, brothers, and grand-aunt came to visit me at the hospital. They were very happy for me, and all told me how much my son looked like his father. I was happy that he was born healthy. That was the most important thing.

We didn't know where Gary was when he was born. My parents called my in-laws to inform them their grandson was born on the Chinese New Year, and that both me and my son were safe and sound. It took his parents three days to find Gary. He called me right away after he heard the news but said he couldn't come to Hong Kong immediately to see us because there were no available flights, which I was surprised to hear. I didn't challenge him or ask why, though. I was tired from the birth, and I didn't care whether he showed up or not. It didn't matter to me. All I cared about was that I had a son, my son.

My marriage at that point was just a piece of paper. I didn't dislike Gary, and I was sure he felt the same—we were still friendly to each other. But we talked mostly about business, or just simple day-to-day matters. We didn't share our feelings; everything stayed on the surface. And there was no real love. I didn't think we knew what it was. Both of us were bound by tradition and a sense of obligation. Besides, we didn't want to shame our parents. So we put up with it.

Gary finally did show up a few days later, and he was pleased to see his son, who looked identical to him—even their birthmarks were in the same places. He was happy and couldn't wait to show his parents their grandson. My son was the first-born male grandson in his family and Gary was proud.

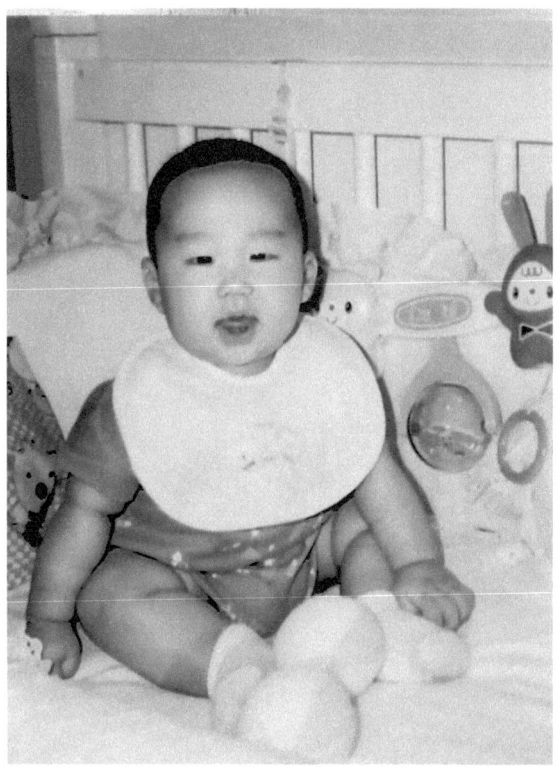

My son, Al, when he was eight months old
- Taipei, Taiwan, 1989

We spent most of Albert's first three years in Taiwan. I hired a full-time nanny to help me to look after him while I worked or travelled. Much of daily life went on as before—I went to work and enjoyed pouring myself into this as I always had—but at the end of the day, I now got to come home to play with my boy. He was adorable. I loved being his mother.

Al and me, at our home when he was only four months old. I was a very happy mom - Taipei, Taiwan, 1989

His grandfather on his father's side was particularly proud to show him off to his friends and clients. When we would go to his office, he would pick him up and put him on his lap while talking business. I had never seen him do anything like that before. People weren't even allowed to enter his office when he was in a meeting. On our son's first- year birthday, which in the Chinese custom is considered an important birthday, he threw him a big party where he invited many friends, family members, and customers to attend. It was a joyful moment for all of us.

When Albert was old enough to travel, I would take him with me, and we travelled to Hong Kong, Singapore, the US, and other countries for work and holidays. I was such a happy mom. We were inseparable. Gary, on the other hand, was out even more—now that our son was home to keep me company, he felt even more carefree in doing what he wanted. My initial thoughts that he might be more settled and spend more time at home after our baby was born were just a fantasy.

Gary told me, "He will be sleeping anyway whether I am home or not. And he will keep you company at night."

I didn't want to argue with him; it was useless.

I wasn't sure if he was having an affair with another woman, and one day, after Mike warned me a woman who worked at the karaoke place was very attentive to him, I did confront Gary. He denied it right away. And I figured, what was the point to even think about it, unless I had evidence? I didn't even care. I had no hurt feelings inside of me and I wasn't angry, so I let it go. It didn't matter to me. I had my son, a beautiful, lovely, cute, and adorable boy, who gave me love and a purpose in my life.

Al was six years old here. We are always happy
- a trip to US, 1995

Al and me on another trip to the US - 1995

I didn't know what it felt like to have an intimate love relationship. I hadn't seen that in my parents either—there was no kissing or touching or staring into the other's eyes like we saw in movies. I had boyfriends when I was younger, but they felt more like a companion to do cool things with than a passionate love. What was romantic love? How did it feel? I wondered. But I was content enough without it. There was so much else in my life, and at the time, I thought it was enough.

I continued to be very busy with work, both managing my family's business and looking after Gary's family business in China. I was constantly looking for new business opportunities.

When my brother John returned from Japan, where he had spent a few years studying the language, he introduced me to his friend, Michael, who had experience working for a Fortune 500 company in the US as chief financial officer. Michael was Eurasian and looking to return to Asia where he was born. John thought there might be an opportunity for him to come and work for us.

When Michael and I met, he was clearly a very smart and experienced person. I was intrigued by his knowledge as well as his connections; it was very different from working in a family business. I was always fascinated by new ideas and opportunities and wanted to understand how a big company operated. I thought perhaps Michael might be a source of that if we brought him into the family business. He was also good with numbers. We needed to have a good financial person on our team to understand our numbers and cost structure as well as a good lawyer who could advise us on legal matters. After meeting, I agreed with John—Michael could be a great asset to our business.

I was excited but needed to first sell the idea to my family. Hiring someone who wasn't a family member to oversee our financial matters was not a common practice for a traditional Chinese business. It would require a level of open-mindedness.

Over dinner that evening, I spoke to my father and my brothers. They had questions and there was a lot of hesitation at first, but I was determined this was the way we needed to go in order to grow our business and I persisted. Finally, they agreed, but cautioned me to look further into his background and past experiences before making an offer. I was relieved, happy at the same time that my family agreed to it.

When I invited Michael to come work for us, he agreed but requested to only answer to me and no one else in the family. I wasn't too surprised—family businesses did have their disadvantages. Everyone seemed to always have their own opinion. Being a girl in a traditional family, I was lucky my voice and opinion were heard most of the time. Or maybe I was lucky that I was always determined to get what I wanted by backing it up with logical reasons.

After Michael joined us, we successfully expanded our business, acquiring similar businesses in the market. We travelled consistently to the US, China, and Europe, as well as to Southeast Asia, Israel, and the Middle East. He was always very resourceful. When we had a new project, he would draw upon his contacts to introduce me to the right people. We worked well as a team, and he taught me a lot, especially about how international businesses were run.

My work world was opening up more and more. We organized a meeting between a Chinese minister and the French minister to discuss the possibility of opening up tourism in both countries, which was exciting. And by the end of 1996, we had built four plants in China.

Soon, it was time for our son to go to preschool.

He didn't like it at first, and like many young children, he cried when he knew we were going to leave him at the school with other kids. It was a stressful moment for me and for him. It was heart-wrenching for me to see him sobbing, pulling away from the teacher. I told him I would come back very soon, and I was told he settled fast after I left. It didn't take long for him to get used to the school, and after a few weeks, he was looking forward to going.

Because of my work schedule, I had our driver to pick him up, which he loved because "Uncle Xiao Lee" would buy him a snack and a drink after school. Xiao Lee became a good friend of my son, and years later I found out he took him on his motorbike to ride around town. If I would have known then, I would have stopped it. Protecting my son was essential to me.

In everything I did, I would think about my son. Motherhood was such an incredible gift to me and I enjoyed every moment of it.

As a mother, I felt wanted and loved, and I was eager to give back my love to him. Being a mother helped me begin to understand what love was all about. I was learning that it gave purpose and fulfillment in life. Albert gave my life a meaning and purpose that I had never had before.

When he was old enough to enter kindergarten, I decided to put him in school in Hong Kong, and so he and I split our time between Hong Kong and Taiwan. Mike's and Barry's children were only one or two years apart in age from Albert and I felt he would benefit growing up with his cousins, especially since he was an only child and they loved him. Besides, I missed my family; it was lonely in Taiwan, much as if I was a single parent.

At first, we went back to Taiwan very often but as Albert started his primary school, it became difficult to leave all the time. Gary would sometimes come to Hong Kong to spend the weekend with us, and sometimes his father would join. It didn't occur to me this was not what a family should be, separated in two different places so often. Yet it worked better for me. If I stayed in Taiwan, I was alone most of the time, but in Hong Kong, I had a whole family to support me.

Gary and I still didn't behave as a married couple. We cared for each other like friends would do—there was no passion or love. And our conversation was always one-sided. I would tell him what our son had done, what he was learning.

He also had no idea how to act as a father. I would have to tell him what he should do and how he should react. "Hold him up, give him a kiss," I would say.

I thought of leaving him many times, but each time when I thought about how our son would lose his father, I would change track. Besides, I was getting my fulfillment from my work, my son, and my family, and thought perhaps that trade-off was my destiny.

Then one day I was at my office in Hong Kong working on a project when the phone rang.

It was Gary. "Would you come back to Taiwan to take care of your son? He won't let me go out at night. He's crying." His voice was panicked.

I had left Albert in Taiwan with Gary for a couple of days, hoping they would spend some quality time together without me around. "It's just a couple of nights," I said. "Could you just stay with him?"

"Oh . . . I can't. I have business to discuss with friends," he said.

I was angry. "Can't you just stay with him? It won't kill you to not go out for a night or two! And don't you dare leave him there by himself . . ."

"Please come back. I can't handle him," he said. Then the phone died.

I booked the earliest morning flight out to Taiwan and brought my son back to Hong Kong the same day. When I got to Taiwan, my son told me he had gotten up in the middle of the night before and there was no one in the house. He had jumped into our big bed and hidden, covering his little body with the sheet and blanket. His father came back in the morning.

He was so scared.

I was angry and horrified to hear of this. I thought, What kind of father would leave a six-year-old child in the house by himself in the middle of the night?

I found out later that Gary had our driver Xiao Lee stay with our son until he fell asleep, and afterwards, Xiao Lee left to go home, thinking Gary would return soon.

I didn't care whether Gary had asked the driver to stay. I couldn't believe a father could be so irresponsible.

I felt violated, disgusted, hurt, angry, and heartbroken. Most of all, I felt betrayed by a man who would behave this way toward his own son. All the feelings that I had suppressed inside of me for years now surfaced. It was like a sleeping volcano had finally erupted.

By this point, our marriage only existed because of our child—it was the only thing that was left to hold us together. If he as a father couldn't even manage the basic responsibility of a parent to protect his own child, what was the point of having such a parent? I'd also recently found out that he was in fact having an affair, and now everything was broken. There was nothing left of our marriage.

I felt like I was waking up from a bad dream, only it wasn't a dream—it was real. Everything became clear to me. I realized I had been in denial for all those years. I had never had a marriage. I was just hanging in there hoping it would be okay.

But after ten years, I was finally admitting this was a wrong marriage from the start. Nothing would make it right, not even our son.

Why had I been holding onto it all this time? Was there fear that I didn't want to confront? Or was I too comfortable to change, even if it was hurting me? At least this hurt was familiar. Was stepping into the unknown scarier than feeling the pain?

Whatever it was, this time it was different. The pain was stronger than anything, and I could no longer ignore it. I felt it deep in my heart and it wasn't just my pain. My son was hurting.

I could picture the terrified moment of him being alone, not knowing what to do. The fear inside of him. That was enough to wake me up and face the reality.

This was not a marriage that I wanted to hold on to. There would be no miracle that would make things right. I was not my mother, not of a generation that felt you could only suffer till the end and live with it.

I tried for ten years; I did what I thought I could. I put everything else before myself, living in an illusion with the hope one day things would turn out right. And now I thought, who am I kidding? There was nothing there to begin with. I kept asking myself, Why am I holding on to this marriage, putting everything else first except my own happiness? Was I afraid if I left, people would judge me as foolish because they thought I had a good marriage? Was I afraid to lose the freedom I had, the freedom to travel, to do what I wanted except for being loved?

Why didn't I act on this earlier? I asked myself. What was I waiting for? I realized the answer was simple—I was too afraid to change. I didn't know what love in marriage was, and instead, I had filled this hole with work and material things. And because of this, I felt an emptiness inside; the loneliness and desire to be loved was never met.

I kept asking myself, "Do you want to spend the rest of your life living this way? What kind of example are you showing to your son?"

It was 1997. I knew I did have choices in my life, and I no longer wanted to choose this.

I picked up the phone to call my lawyer. "Hi, Stephen," I said. "I want to file for a divorce."

Chapter 5

THE BREAKUP OF TWO FAMILIES

At first, I kept the divorce to myself, not even telling my family. I didn't want to be influenced by anyone, to be told what I should do or shouldn't do. This was the first time in my life I was very clear about what I wanted to do. My son was the reason for my determination.

I also understood it would be a process to prepare everything before we even served the papers to Gary. My lawyer and I needed to determine what grounds I would use for the divorce and we needed to decide where I should file.

The most important thing in my divorce was to make sure I had custody of my son, and this couldn't be taken for granted. In the Taiwan legal system, custody was often given to the father because it was still a male-dominant society. In my case, it would be even more difficult to win custody in Taiwan because of the status of Gary's family. It took me a while to weigh all the pros and cons before I decided the best place to file was in Hong Kong. Although I could also do it in the US, it was too far for me to travel while I was still handling the family business.

Stephen, who was my good friend as well as my lawyer, helped me put all the facts together and compile the necessary argument. It was a complicated and often overwhelming undertaking, as there was no jurisdiction between Hong Kong and Taiwan. The whole process took almost a year to prepare.

Then in 1998, we were ready, and the divorce papers were served to Gary at our home in Taiwan.

As I was working on the divorce case, I was also very busy with the family business. We were working on a big project that had been underway for almost ten years— taking the company public. It was an exciting time for the family, Mike and I were working closely on it together.

The amount of work involved in the process was enormous, because neither Mike nor I had done this before. We put a team of people together to work on it. One day, Mike brought in a manager from Southeast Asia whom he'd met through a friend; he thought he would be the ideal person to run the operation.

I had been taking the lead on the operation initially and had questions about this person's ability and creditability, especially as I was not consulted on this. Mike thought he had experience that I might not have. It was true I had never done an IPO before but I wasn't sure this other person had the experience either. No one had checked into his background or experience, and so I thought it was a reckless decision.

This person joined the company despite my doubts and things went badly. The team was confused and wouldn't follow his instructions. It turned out that he definitely did not have the capability or the leadership we needed.

He brought in an investor from Singapore whom I was not comfortable with. They talked big, but they certainly didn't look professional to me. When I went to Mike to caution him on this, he told me to leave it to him, that he knew what he was doing. I didn't feel good about this at all. It was so clear to me something wasn't right. The investor wanted Mike to sign a document that didn't seem to protect our interest in the company, and when I had our lawyer review it, I was told to be very careful. When I told Mike about this, he ignored me, and once again asked me to leave it to him. I thought we should at least discuss this as a family and I was angry. "You are making a mistake!" I said. He didn't listen.

I had no way to make him change his mind. The only person who could stop him was my father.

I went to see him right away and explained the situation. I asked my father to let me take it over. I had initiated the project and I was confident I could do it. I also had a good team of people working on it. The project was a big part of our business, I said, and it was too risky to partner with someone we knew nothing about. I told my father we needed to think it through, that we could lose a lot if we weren't careful.

My father's reply shocked me. He simply said, "Let your brother make the decision."

I protested. "Dad, he is about to fall off a cliff. We're supposed to just watch him without helping?"

"He is your brother, your older brother. Let him make the decision," he said.

I couldn't believe what I'd heard. Yes, he was my older brother, and I loved him, but he was not doing the right thing. And this decision could affect everyone in the family. All my life, I thought we were a team, that I was an equal among my brothers. I had been proud of being a girl in a traditional family because I was treated the same. I never felt I was given less—in fact, most of the time, I got more than my brothers. And I gave a lot back; I worked hard, and all my decisions sought to put the family first.

But listening to my father, I felt his mistrust. I felt he had doubts about my ability to handle the work, and worst of all, I felt it was because I was "the girl" in the family. That day I suddenly realized that while my father loved me, he didn't trust me in the same way as he did my brothers. I was merely a daughter, a supporter, and my opinion was not as important because I was a girl. I had always been confident, thanks to my parents who taught me to be strong. After speaking with my father, I felt hurt and no longer like a part of the team.

I went home, demoralized, lost, and trying hard to make sense of what had just happened. The conversation with my dad replayed over and over in my head. What am I going to do? I asked myself.

I knew if I stayed in the family business, I wouldn't be happy, knowing my decisions didn't matter, knowing there was no trust in my ability to handle things. This would make my work and life miserable—I knew I would end up fighting with my brothers all the time. I loved them all; they were a huge part of my life, my family. All of this—how I now felt about our work together and my place in it—would damage our relationship, and I didn't want to see that.

I thought about this hard. Ultimately, I knew I could either stay in the business and do what I was told or leave the family business and keep our relationship. I knew what was best for us—for me to leave the business and keep peace.

I told Mike he could take things over, that I didn't want to be involved in the business anymore.

I didn't think too much about my future. Whatever would happen, I would deal with it.

When I called Stephen and told him, he was shocked. "May," he said. "You have just filed for divorce and you're leaving the family business at the same time? Have you thought about how you are going to support yourself and your son? You'll have no money from Gary until the court decides on the case—it could be a few years. Why don't you stay in the business while your divorce is settled, and handle the rest later? Then you'll have some income."

"No, I would rather deal with all the bad things at one time instead of dealing with them one by one," I said. "I will be alright."

Once I filed the papers, Gary's father wanted to meet with me.

We'd chosen the tearoom at the Peninsula Hotel in Hong Kong. It was a popular place for locals and tourists to enjoy English high tea in the afternoon, and that day it was filled with people.

I sat in the corner near a sunny window. When I saw Gary's father walk in from the main entrance of the hotel, I waved at him, and he walked toward my table. He looked a little tired but still looked sharp in his well-pressed suit and tie.

"How was the flight?" I asked him.

"Okay," he said.

I called the waiter and ordered his tea of choice, Earl Grey with lemon for him.

Then he asked me, "What happened to you and Gary? I didn't expect this."

"Dad," I replied, "this has been going on for a long time. Our marriage isn't working. I wanted it to work too but at this point I'm exhausted trying anymore, and nothing works between us. I've tried too many times. He's having an affair, and now he's not being responsible as a father. This is the right choice."

He looked at me and I could see his mind thinking over how to respond. "I know he is not a perfect husband; he has lots of faults, but he is not a bad person. The affair is just a businessman thing, nothing serious. I will make sure it won't happen again. I know I can change him—you give me two years or even one, and if I can't change him, you can do whatever you want."

I didn't know why we were having this conversation—I was married to his son, not him—but Gary was nowhere to be seen. Ever since my lawyer had handed him the divorce papers, he hadn't called me or his son. And now here I was with his father.

This shouldn't come as a surprise to me, I thought to myself. In the last ten years of our marriage, every time we had a problem it was always his dad or mom who would come to talk to me first, asking me to forgive him or telling me they didn't teach their son the right way, that it was their fault. They would apologize to me. I used to hate this so much, but it became enough of a pattern that I became used to it.

"Dad, I could give you two years, five years, but it wouldn't change my decision. I could wait but he is not going to change. And my decision has been made. I'm sorry."

The look in his eyes changed. He was definitely angry now. He sat taller, took a sip of his tea, then spoke. His voice became businesslike—I knew that tone too well. "So, what do you want?"

That was direct, I thought. "All I need is for Gary to take care of his son's education and a roof over our head." That's what I asked for, nothing else.

In traditional Chinese families, the men usually took care of the family's expenses. The children's education was normally paid for by the family and even the houses we lived in were usually under the family name and not our own. We didn't have anything that was considered solely ours.

And so his reply shocked me.

"If you want money, you come back to work for me," he said.

I couldn't believe what I heard. By working for him, it was clear to me he also meant staying in the marriage. He wanted to keep us together enough that he would refuse to offer any support otherwise. Suddenly things fell into place in my mind. He was trying to negotiate with me now. And I saw that this had been a business marriage from the start.

My brain went back to the night before the wedding when Gary was questioning why we were even together. He'd also once told me that his dad liked me, that his dad had asked him to pursue me. I had jokingly replied that I was married to him and not his dad. But now I could see his dad's hand in everything—his dad wanting me to be a part of his business.

I started to think about how soon after Gary and I got married his dad said he wanted his business to expand into China, and in order to do so, they needed the help of someone they trusted who had the means to enter China. China was just opening to the outside world then and not everyone was comfortable in the country or had connections there. Who could be better than me or my family? I would make it all easier, especially since I was a businesswoman who understood how business was done.

Everything was so clear to me.

Gary had never been in love with me, like I was probably never in love with him. I had gone along with our marriage because at the time, I didn't really understand what love was. And he had proposed because his father wanted him to. To him, being an obedient son was the most important thing.

I now understand why he had been so unhappy. Going out every night was a way to release his unhappiness, a way to escape. This didn't give him an excuse to be an irresponsible husband and father, but I felt I understood him better.

What a fool I was, I thought. Why hadn't I seen that before?

I stood up and went to the ladies' room. I couldn't hold my tears back anymore; they rolled down my cheeks like an unstoppable river.

I was hurt and angry. I felt betrayed, like I had been taken advantage of.

It had never crossed my mind that I was being used as a business deal.

I was angry at myself too, thinking of how stupid I was. I had never been deep in love in this marriage. Why had I gone along with it?

After staying in the ladies' room for I don't know how long, I tidied myself up and walked back to the table. I tried to look as normal as I possibly could.

After I sat down, I immediately called for the check, paid it, and stood up.

We didn't continue our conversation. I couldn't.

We walked together silently out of the hotel.

I called for a taxi and asked, "Do you want me to go to the airport with you?"

"No," he said, matter-of-factly.

"Are you sure?" I said.

"I will be fine," he replied. That was the last time we talked as a father and daughter-in-law.

Once the papers were filed and I'd spoken with my father-in-law, I told my mother.

As I explained to her why I was leaving and couldn't stay in the marriage anymore, she was very calm, as if she had known this for a long time. Then she asked me, "Are you sure you want to do this? This will be your own decision. I can't tell you what you should or should not do."

I was a little uncomfortable with her reply. I had expected her to comfort me, to be on my side, to feel sorry for me. To perhaps say something like, "Yes, I think this is all too much. I am so sorry you've had to go through this." Instead, I was questioned about my decision.

I remembered the time when I told my mother I was going to marry Gary. She asked me then, "Are you sure he is the one? Do you really want to marry him? It will be your own decision." I told her then, "I like him, and yes, he is the one."

This time my reply to her was no different. "This is my decision," I said. "I will take full responsibility. From the beginning I wanted to marry him and now I want to divorce him. This is my own decision, no one else's."

As I said this, I still felt a bit angry about her reaction. Deep down, I was scared and I wanted the comfort of my mother telling me it would be alright, that she would be there to protect me. But I knew she was from an old school. She loved me very much, but she also knew that I needed to be strong. In her mind, I needed to build my strength and courage so that no matter what came my way, I would be able to fight through it. Comforting me would make me rely on her, and I wouldn't then have the courage to find my own way out.

This was what she'd taught me over a lifetime—make your own decision and take full responsibility for the outcome, whether it was good or bad. This was how she held herself.

I got a lot from my mother—she was a fighter. She had to be to survive as an outsider in my father's family in order to make sure her children would be alright. That was what was important to her, and she made it happen. It was a traditional cultural way of thinking that she had grown up with.

I knew I was a fighter too. I had always been. I knew I would always find a way through, no matter how hard something might seem or how much fear I had inside.

We were both fighters and yet we'd also both grown up in a traditional culture and put others' happiness ahead of our own. I had done that for almost my whole life. The difference between us was that I was then realizing I had choices in my life, even in areas I thought were fixed. No matter how hard or scary the unknown might be, there were choices.

As I made this choice for myself, she wanted to help me continue learning to be strong. She knew I would need that.

My mother and me, during one of her visits to
Taipei - Taiwan, 1996

After I told my mother, I told others in my family while we gathered at our seaside home. My brother Mike responded by saying I hadn't tried hard enough.

I couldn't believe what I heard. My anger was fast and I couldn't hold in my feelings. "What do you know about my marriage?" I said. "Over the years, I have never come home to cry or to complain about it. You have no right to judge me. You are not me. You don't know what I have gone through. Why don't you just be happy for me that I've chosen to leave something unhappy?" I went on and on.

My father was sitting next to Mike and didn't say anything. How could he? He was also betraying my mother.

I stormed out of the room and went downstairs to get my car keys. Before I left, I heard them still talking about me. "Don't push her, let her think it through. You know she has a strong will," my dad told him.

I knew they were thinking that what I was going through may be hurtful, but that didn't mean we should divorce. In my family, no one had ever gone through a divorce.

As long as the men in my family still looked after everyone by putting food on the table and providing a roof for shelter, they considered themselves responsible husbands. They were fulfilling their duty. The woman's duty on the other hand was to look after the children and take care of the house. I didn't depend on Gary to bring money and food home. I earned it myself from working in the business. Our marriage was not a trading—it should have been about love, happiness, growth, taking care of each other and supporting each other as parents.

My father and Mike didn't see it this way, though. Unfortunately, in our culture there was still a certain expectation for a woman, to obey, be submissive. Some women themselves thought they didn't deserve to have happiness, like my mother. I was this woman once too. When my marriage didn't go as I expected—when it became clear we didn't have love for each other—I first went into a denial mode and used work and travelling as my escape, keeping myself busy to avoid thinking about it. It was a trade-off for me, and it worked okay for a while. Then when my son Albert came into my life, I began to understand what love was all about. I could feel it; it became part of me. I wanted to protect him from anything that might harm him. And when he was treated poorly by his own father who was supposed to do the same, I knew there was nothing else left. It was like waking up from a bad dream.

And whatever anyone else thought—I knew it was the right choice.

Chapter 6

DEPRESSION

I took Albert away to London for a few days so we could spend some time together away from home. I felt the change would be a good backdrop for what I was about to tell him. Our hotel was centrally located at Knightsbridge, where plenty of restaurants and shops are around. I had always liked London, since my time there as a student, and the place gave me a welcome sense of familiarity.

The day after we arrived, we went out for a big breakfast. Albert and I both enjoyed the English breakfast of tea and toast with fried eggs, bacon, baked beans, and mushroom. Afterwards, we returned to our room for a rest and he lay down.

I was nervous. I had no idea how he would react to what I was about to tell him.

"I have something to tell you," I said, "but I want you to know, it is not your fault. You haven't done anything wrong. I want you to know that."

He looked at me, clearly having no idea what I was talking about.

I continued. "Mom and Dad are going through a divorce right now. Things are not working out for us. I know this might come as a shock to you, but he will always be your father. He loves you, and this will not change."

Tears started to roll down his face. He asked me, "Why?"

I struggled to find the right words. I didn't want to tell him about his father's irresponsibility toward the both of us or that there was another woman in his life. He was too young to understand; he was only eight years old. "Sometimes, things just didn't work out for married people, and it is best for us to find our own way." I wasn't sure what I was saying. I wasn't sure he could understand it—it didn't make much sense to me even but that was the best reason I could come up with.

Clearly, he didn't understand. He was crying. I went over to him and put my hand on his head, trying to comfort him. I was crying too, not because I was leaving his father, but because of the pain I saw in my son. "He is still your dad," I said. "You will still see him, nothing much will change. This is between Mom and Dad; you have nothing to do with this."

I didn't know what else I could say. The guilt started to overwhelm me—I had taken his father away from him. How could I do that to my boy? My heart was hurting even more.

We both were crying together, but somehow, still, I knew this was the right choice.

As the divorce continued, things became very hard.

I had no energy to get up in the morning—there was nowhere I needed to go, no clients I needed to see. So most days, I woke up around noon then went about my day, pretending I was alright. When I was with people, I acted like nothing had happened, talking and laughing. I must be a very good actor. Over time, I didn't even want to be with people anymore. I would find all kinds of excuses to tell my friends why I couldn't go out. After a while, I noticed, my friends didn't call as much. My family, which was the biggest part of my life, also started to distance themselves.

My father still called me every day at first, asking me about the business. "How's the project going?" he would say.

"Dad, I don't know," I would reply. "I don't handle the work anymore." He would continue to ask me many questions about the business, and I played along at first, giving him thoughts about this project and that one, much like I had done in the past. I didn't want him to feel I didn't care anymore. I wanted to care, I wanted to help make things happen, but in reality, I was out of the family business.

One day when he called, I simply told him, "Dad, I don't work in the business anymore, why don't you ask Mike?" He went quiet. I knew this was not what he wanted to hear from me.

I was sure it hurt him so much to know that I wasn't working in the business anymore—he had trained me since I was a young girl. In our work together, I understood him even before he could finish his words. I had never said "no" to him. Like he rarely had to me—this was how he showed his deep love and care for me. He would usually give me anything I wanted. And now, he didn't know how to help me.

I pushed everyone away, including my family. Eventually, no one called to check on me. I was left alone like a child who has cast away. They probably didn't know how to communicate with me because I had always been so strong and independent. I was the one who took care of everyone else, solving their problems and their needs. They just didn't know how they could help. I still saw them sometimes, but not very often. And while I knew they cared, I wished they could be more present and supportive. I felt hurt.

My room became my sanctuary.

The days were long. I didn't know what I was doing most days.

Nights were the hardest part. I couldn't sleep and would curl up on the floor, crying and sobbing. I asked myself, "How did I get to this?" The fear and pain in my heart were so strong it almost paralyzed me. I wondered, What am I supposed to do now?

Putting up a strong face during the years of depression. This was taken in the midst of the divorce - Hong Kong, 1999

Then one day I got a call from a business friend, Frank Rocco, who was in town. He asked if I wanted to get lunch.

I had first met Frank in a business meeting a few years back. Our family chief financial officer, Michael, had introduced us and we became friends. He was an American lawyer with one of the top ten biggest beverage companies in the US, and he'd been assigned to work in Asia with Hong Kong as his base. He travelled constantly. After returning from his trips, Frank would call to catch up; we would have lunch every few months. Frank was a people person, and I enjoyed our time together, mainly because he would talk about his trips and the places that he had visited. Some of them were very remote and I would try to picture what they looked like. I had always been curious about the world, and hearing him talk would bring me into a new world, which was exciting to me. He was also well read in almost any topic that would come up. I was fascinated by the knowledge he had—I always wondered, how did he know so much? He was obviously very smart; I was drawn to him because I admired smart people, as I felt I could learn so much.

This time, the lunch got cancelled because he had an unexpected meeting, so we decided to meet for dinner instead. I normally wouldn't have gone to dinner. I had a belief that as a married businesswoman, going out with a man for lunch was acceptable because the purpose was to build a business relationship and the conversation was mostly business. Dinner would not be appropriate—unless it was a group dinner—because there were no time constraints, people are more relaxed, and conversation focused more on personal events. Besides the fact of being married, I was also quite a private person; therefore, dinner would not be my choice for meeting a business friend. But that day, I decided to do it anyway; after all, I was going through my divorce, I didn't have much business to discuss, and he was a friend whom I had known for some time by then.

We met at a popular Italian restaurant in Central, where every table was occupied. The place was noisy and the energy was high. We both knew the restaurant manager well; it was a comfortable place to meet up. We talked about his recent trip and he wanted to know how my business was doing. After a couple glasses of wine, I felt comfortable sharing with him what was happening in my life, that I had left my family business and was going through a divorce at the same time.

He was shocked but he listened well without making any judgment or comment. He said he was sorry to hear that and asked if there was anything he could do to help. In some way, I felt relieved that I could open up to him. I probably badly needed someone to talk to.

We began to see each other more often after that. I felt a sense of comfort being around him—he was a good listener and he gave me advise that I really needed at times. He could look at an issue logically and not in an emotional way, which I really appreciated and believed probably had something to do with his profession as a lawyer. Being around him gave me a sense of security. I could feel his genuine care, and around him I felt seen and heard, which

I didn't in my marriage. He became the person I went to whenever I had a problem I couldn't solve or needed to get advice on a legal issue in my divorce case. But most importantly he was someone I could easily talk to.

After a few months of getting to know each other better on a personal level, we started dating and our relationship grew. It was a slow and careful approach on my part. I wasn't sure I wanted to jump right into a new relationship, and I also thought about my son. In my traditional mindset at that time, I was more concerned about my son's feelings than my own. Along with this, I also occasionally heard a little voice in my head asking me to be cautious because my feelings might not be real. Maybe they could be coming out of desperation, of badly needing someone to talk to. I was careful about my own feelings; I didn't want to be hurt again. Yet I appreciated his place in my life, even as we took things slowly.

While I felt deep comfort in my growing relationship with Frank, this period was still deeply difficult. I felt no confidence in anything and questioned myself about any decision I made, even small ones. I had tremendous sadness and guilt over what this divorce was doing to my son, who didn't deserve to grow up without a father. It wasn't his choice but a choice I had made for him. "Why am I so selfish? How can I do that to him?" I asked myself.

Alone, I would cry for him. "My poor boy, I am so sorry, I don't deserve to be your mother."

These questions and thoughts repeated in my head again and again. The pain was so strong that some days I would throw up and lie on the bathroom floor for hours and hours, refusing to move or get up to face the reality. This went on for months and months—I don't even know for how long.

As I was in this pain, I also continued living my life. One day I decided to get Lasik eye surgery, which was supposed to be a simple surgery, but I ended up with a fracture on my eyes. I lay in darkness for days, tears running out of them both from the surgery and the pain in my heart. Soon after, I decided to get all four of my wisdom teeth pulled. I got a very good doctor, who assured me it should be a straightforward procedure, but I ended up with multiple bruises over my jaw because the roots of my teeth were so deep. The doctor told me he hadn't expected that. The surgery, which was expected to be one hour, went almost three hours. All his pulling and digging around my teeth was painful, but I was treating it as though I deserved to be punished. I couldn't even get my eyes and teeth fixed right.

Everything I did was wrong; everything I touched was a disaster. My confidence level went from a hundred to almost nonexistent.

I was simply surviving, but I tried to put on a brave face when I was with my son.

The next few years were difficult for Albert. Although he hadn't really spent a lot of time with his father, he at least got to see him when we travelled back to Taiwan during holidays and weekends. But since I filed for divorce, his father had stopped seeing him. At the beginning, he called a few times, but soon, the communication stopped. Occasionally, his grandfather would call him. He assured Albert that the divorce was between Gary and me, that his father still loved him very much. After a while, though, those calls also stopped coming.

I was dealing with my own demons at that time. I was lost. And I didn't know how to listen or talk to Albert. While I sometimes felt tremendous sadness and guilt around what the divorce meant for him, I also had no space in myself to be emotionally present and notice what he was feeling. I had no idea what was going on in his little mind. I also figured there wasn't a lot more to talk about, that he was so young he couldn't understand it all. I would also tell myself that things hadn't changed much—it had always been just me and him most of the time; Gary was seldom there. I didn't think my son would have strong emotions about it like an adult, thinking he probably just wondered why we didn't travel back to Taiwan. I never asked him what he was feeling or how he was doing. It was totally selfish on my part.

The divorce proceedings and resulting custody battle were long and ugly. Because Gary's father was a public figure, the media had a good story to tell, and there was a lot of digging for information about me and my family background. They wanted to know the story behind the divorce, because story sells.

I was not prepared to give them any reason to write about us. I didn't think it was their business, and besides, I was worried about Albert. I even called Gary to tell him that we should keep this to ourselves. Gary's father, though, decided to talk to the media. I'm not sure if it was because of the constant pressure of the media asking him questions or if he felt he had to defend his son. "It was their decision to marry, now they want to divorce," he said. "This young generation is different. When a man goes out to entertain it is all business. I don't understand these young people. One minute they want to get married, the next, they want to divorce. One thing I want her to know—she will not get any money from the company. It belongs to the company. She has no right to touch it."

When I read about the interview, I was angry. It sounded like I filed the divorce because I was after their money. I then decided to accept the newspaper's request for an interview, to tell my story, the truth behind the divorce. I hadn't intended to bring this into the public spotlight, but I didn't have much choice—I certainly didn't want to be portrayed like someone who was after their money. I called the newspaper and they came to Hong Kong to interview me. We had each told our version of the story; the media interpreted it however they wanted. It was on the front page of magazines and newspapers, becoming a soap opera of the time. The funny thing was Gary was nowhere to be seen. All the media was focused on his father and me. I was fighting my divorce with my father-in-law and not my husband.

Gary didn't even show up at court in Hong Kong despite the court summons, probably on the advice of his lawyer. It made it difficult to proceed—the case was dragged on month and month, much longer than it should have been. The hardest part of this was when the court would send someone to talk to my son and ask him questions about his parents. It broke my heart that he had to go through this with a stranger—it was hard enough for him already. I had asked the court not to do this, but it was part of the divorce procedure to determine the custody for my son.

To make things even more complicated, Gary had filed a separate divorce case in Taiwan, hoping to get custody of our son. I was now facing two divorce cases in two separate countries. In Taiwan law, custody was more likely to go to Gary, especially because of his family influence. I was determined to do whatever it took to keep my son. I knew there would be no future for my child if he ended up with his father, an irresponsible father.

During those years, fighting for custody was my only goal in life; nothing else mattered to me. I went to court many times, giving my affidavit as evidence, and not once did I see Gary. After two and a half years of this case being dragged out, the court finally gave a verdict—I was awarded full custody of my son and a handsome alimony. We sent the verdict to Taiwan through my local lawyer, arguing there was already a decision in Hong Kong. The local court there decided to put the case on hold, hoping to find a solution. I thought that was the end of it, that my son and I could move on with our life. But when I tried to enforce the alimony, I was faced with another challenge.

There was no divorce jurisdiction between Taiwan and Hong Kong, and therefore, the court ruling couldn't be executed in Taiwan.

Gary definitely didn't want to pay me or my son for anything. Whenever I tried to enforce the judgment, I was met with all kinds of laws that prohibited me from carrying it out, with lawyers citing there were no preexisting cases of its kind before mine. I was left with no support from Gary, at the same time that I had exhausted most of my savings in the divorce battle and was still faced with mountain of bills and school fees that I had to pay. A part of me was relieved that the divorce was finally over but facing the future without any financial support at all was another challenge.

I didn't know what the future would hold. But I was determined to not let this affect my son. I knew I could continue filing for legal action against Gary for not paying the alimony, but it would be another long process. And it might involve my son in the matter, which I was trying hard to avoid. The most important thing was to have my son with me.

I was left, though, with many questions about the future, very little money in the bank, and the fear of not being able to pay for my son's education.

I didn't tell Albert what was going on because I didn't want him to worry; in my mind, he was too young to understand, and this was my way of protecting him. His job was to study hard and not worry about anything else. I was very much a traditional mother in this way; we didn't talk much about our feelings. My mother never did to me until a much later stage of her life.

When I was with my son, I put on a strong face, but deep down, I was afraid and confused. I didn't know how to support the lifestyle we had always had or how to pay for his education. I still had some money left, but it wouldn't last long. I had no income from my family and no way to get my alimony.

Yet even with the pressure I was facing, I still couldn't bring myself to go find a job. I didn't know what I could do.

My excuse was that I had never really worked for other people in my life aside from the sales job I did while in England. But the reality was that I was ashamed to work for others; my ego rejected it. I used to be a boss and everyone knew that I came from a good family. What was I going to tell people? "Oh yes, I've been my own boss for the last fifteen years, but I had a fight with my family, so I left." Did this even make sense? How would people look at me?

I was ashamed and had no confidence. I couldn't start a business because I had no money. I kept telling myself how I couldn't do this, or I couldn't do that. I turned into a negative person, with one excuse after another.

Where was the old me? The one who wasn't afraid of anything, who felt nothing could stop me? That confidence was all gone. I was afraid of everything and doubted my ability to do anything except hide at home.

I started selling my jewelry to pay for my son's school fees and our living expenses. I knew if it came down to it and we needed to feed ourselves, I could always go back to my family. But my pride was too high to ask for any help.

I was financially broke, with no sense of where I was going and how I could make money to pay for anything. I felt like I had fallen to the bottom of my life, and I couldn't see any hope in front of me. I felt all alone, scared, and hopeless. My self-esteem was totally gone, and I was back to crying every day, wishing God would give me a miracle, to save me. Some days I would feel a little better, but it didn't last long, and then I was back to the hole again.

But despite all the fear and uncertainty, I never regretted what I did. Deep down, even as I didn't see hope directly in front of me, I knew I would find a way to climb back up again. It was a matter of when. My gut feeling told me this. This had all been my decision, and I had to take full responsibility. I had to live with it or find a way to get out of it. But it was easier said than done. I was my own worst enemy as I told myself excuse after excuse.

I was so afraid how others would judge me, I still pretended I was okay, even in front of my own family.

The only people that I could talk to about how I felt during this time were Frank and my friends Don and Janie Dunlap, whom I had met at the Taiwan cocktail party years before. After my marriage, we had become very close. Don had helped me tremendously in my business ventures in the US and introduced me to many businessmen and politicians, all of whom expanded my worldview. Janie had taught me so much about love and care; she had been a housewife since she had married Don, and her whole life had been about family and taking care of them. A kindhearted woman who had been raised in South Carolina, she treated me like her own daughter. I visited them at least twice a year, always staying at their home. I would even keep some of my clothes there so I didn't have to bring any when I visited them. We travelled together constantly, even after my son was born, and they loved and cared for us both like family. They were like my "American parents," and I had trusted and confided in them with personal issues, especially around my marriage. In this new period of difficulty, Don and Janie listened, encouraged me, and gave me comfort. Because of them and Frank, I knew I was still cared for.

One day, I received a small pamphlet by mail that was sent by Janie. It was a prayer from her local church that encouraged people who had gone through divorce, talking of how to build a new life and how God is always there to love them. I couldn't stop crying. In that moment, I felt so much love around me and holding me. It was a moment in my life that I will never forget.

I believe the biggest fear in life is that we won't be loved. And in that period of fear and worry, this pamphlet from Janie showed me so much love, I began to slowly let that fear go.

The love I felt during that time was the love I had been for which I had been longing for so long. Frank, Don, and Janie helped me truly understand what love was, what it was to feel loved, and how powerful it can be. They helped me understand that it was not money or things that mattered; it was love that we need.

For this, I am forever thankful to them.

I continued to struggle with my confidence. I also continued to miss my family. The shift from seeing them every day to seeing them less and less was hard for me.

I knew I had made the right decision leaving the family business; I didn't regret it. But at the same time, I began asking myself, What was the real reason that I left? Did I really know? Was it really because my father wouldn't let me be in charge of the project? Or that he wouldn't trust me to be able to handle it? Or was it more that my expectation of love from my family wasn't met? Was I so full of myself that when things didn't go my way, I threw a tantrum like a child?

As I searched for my own answers to these questions, Frank continued to be there for me. I was still crying all the time and didn't have interest in doing much. He kept encouraging me to try something new, but my confidence was so low I kept rejecting his ideas. He knew I had the ability to do things, but I didn't see it myself any longer. I saw my failures instead. My son was struggling, and in addition to it possibly being because he was unhappy without a father, I also wondered if it was because his mom had a new boyfriend. Frank was patient, understanding it might not be easy for my son, and let things happen in their time.

It was a bit hard for both of them at first. Frank was trying his best to be the male figure he needed in his life, while my son didn't understand why this man was in his life and wasn't sure he could share his own feelings with anyone. But they tried. Frank took him to games, talked to him about American culture, and they even travelled together. While it was difficult sometimes, over time my son came to see him as someone who cared for both him and his mother. His own father had disappeared after the divorce, and that had a big impact on him. Having Frank around did fill some of the gaps that were missing in my son's growing up. It wasn't perfect all the time, but there was genuine care and love on both sides. And Frank was trying everything he could to make us feel comfortable, not pushing me or telling my son what to do.

He was there so that I had a shoulder to lean on. I couldn't imagine anyone would do that for me. I dumped so much onto him that I am ashamed even just thinking about it now, but I needed him, and he was there. This was something I had never experienced, the feeling of having someone give me so much love in this way. I was beginning to understand how it felt to be loved by someone, not just physically but mentally too. He taught me how to love.

During the time when I lost most of my confidence, I was full of excuses. The voice in my head was so strong that it took control of me. You are not good enough . . . what experience do you have . . . where do you find the money . . . who would hire you . . . what do people think about you . . . you don't have help . . . you can't do this . . . They went on and on, and each time opportunity presented itself, I just pushed it away.

I went about doing things that didn't require me to be with people. I didn't want to look them in the eyes—I felt I knew what they thought of me. I was hiding most of the time.

It became my habit very soon. It felt comfortable and familiar even though this hiding also created anxiety in me.

Frank encouraged me every chance he had but my answer was always the same. I didn't have this, I didn't have that, I couldn't do it because . . . It was a miracle that he didn't leave me. It must have been difficult to be with someone who had so much negative energy. He knew I had the ability to do anything I wanted, but sadly, I couldn't see it myself. It was all fear—fear to try, fear to fail, fear to lose face, fear to be looked down at by others, fear about myself!

I took him for granted, and he was so patient with me. I was sure he was hurting inside too. So were the other people around me, including Albert. I tried to put up a strong front with my son, but in reality, I didn't even know what I was doing. I was constantly fighting within myself. There was a force that kept pulling me back each time I wanted to break through.

Frank had been asking me to set a date for our wedding ever since my divorce was finalized, but I kept pushing and delaying. A big part of me wasn't sure I wanted to commit to another relationship so fully right after my divorce, even though the divorce had taken so long. I was scared—what if this didn't work? I loved Frank, and I knew he loved me very much, but I had a fear of losing the love. I had a lot of uncertainty around the idea that love could actually last, which led to my having no confidence in marriage.

After dating for almost four years, I finally agreed to set a date.

I remember the day I told my son. We were driving home and I said, "Mom is going to get married to Frank. What do you think?"

He answered me in a very mature way for a twelve-year-old that surprised me. "As long as you are happy, you should go for it. BUT—he can't tell me what to do." I laughed but I also worried, Will they get along? I hoped so. But I still was scared of moving forward.

But as the date approached, we didn't do anything. We hadn't invited anyone or made any wedding arrangements. Just about a month before the wedding date, at Frank's request, we went to see a psychologist. Frank thought it might help me or give me some answers regarding my reluctance.

We walked into a clinic in Central, a financial district of Hong Kong, both of us dressed professionally. He wore a suit and a tie, and I was wearing a black dress. We sat down and the psychologist, a woman in her forties, asked how we were doing and what seemed to be the problem.

I was quite open about my feelings, including my loss of confidence when I left the family business. She listened attentively, then asked Frank, "How do you feel about this?"

Frank responded that he loved me very much, but he also felt like a crutch to me. He said he didn't know what to do. He had tried to find ways to help me but he had failed. He felt lost too.

I was totally surprised by how he felt. As I listened to him express his frustration that he didn't know how to help me, I began crying uncontrollably. I was so ashamed of myself. I had no clue I had put him in such a situation. I was sad and also angry at myself. The psychologist tried to comfort me, but I knew at that point, the only person who could help me was me!

I suddenly realized it was all wrong, that I was being so selfish, hurting myself and those I loved so dearly. How could I do that?

What did my parents teach me? I heard the voice of my mother. "Be responsible in what you do." I had forgotten what that meant.

As I sat in shame and anger, I thought, I've had enough of this! I am better than this.

I should have been celebrating because it was my decision to leave, and I was free to pursue anything I wanted, but that's not what I had been doing. I was supposed to be responsible for my own decisions—it was how I was brought up—but instead I was just blaming this and that. Where was the old me?

I left our session with a new awareness, and new questions.

When I had the courage to start looking inward, to understand what I really wanted, I realized what was lacking in my life, what was stopping me from doing what I wanted. It wasn't the absence of money or opportunity. There was no external obstacle in my way.

What was stopping me was the absence of loving myself and believing in love. I was paralyzed because I was afraid of doing anything that would confirm my fear that I wasn't good enough or put me in a position where I could lose love.

My parents didn't have a good relationship in their marriage—they were together because it was an obligation and cultural expectation. Their definition of love was to be with each other till the end even though there was no love. Gary had never given me love, because he had only married me because of his father. Ours was marriage in which love didn't exist. I was hurt when my father chose my brother over me to handle the business because he was the oldest child. For me, it felt like a loss in love from my father.

These experiences had left their mark on me.

The new anger I'd felt made me confront myself. I was doing the same thing to those I loved, by pushing them away. When I began to realize how love had played a big role in what was lacking in my life, I asked myself, What about those who want and need my love? Have I been falling into the same trap of not knowing how to love them? Have I truly given my love to those I care for and love dearly? I thought of Albert and Frank. I had been so preoccupied with finding my way back to myself, I hadn't paid enough attention to them. I didn't want to continue this way.

I was ready to start stepping more into love. We began planning our wedding.

Chapter 7

A NEW BEGINNING

We had the most beautiful wedding in a small Italian restaurant in Hong Kong. Frank and I invited around a hundred people, both family and friends, and I got to involve myself in every little detail, from our guests to the decorations and table arrangements, the menu and the wine, even down to what kind of pens our guests would use to sign in. In my first wedding, I hadn't chosen anything and hadn't had a bridal party. This time was different. People who meant something to us were a part of our day. I asked my close friend Sue to be my bridesmaid. She was the daughter of one of my American friends and had lived with me for six months as she explored Asia. She and her boyfriend Kevin flew in from Louisiana to attend our wedding.

Frank and I were so happy. It was a memorable day for us. The love and care I felt from my husband—I had never known this could exist.

Frank and me on our wedding day, together with my parents
- Hong Kong, 2002

We had married. I had stepped forward into love. I knew I didn't want to let fear keep me from moving forward in the rest of my life either, and yet I was still afraid.

Things were also difficult with Albert. Over the past years, his behavior had been slowly changing. Now a young teenager, he looked angry most of the time, and would talk back to me if I said something he didn't like. He would go out with friends and not come home until late. I had no idea where he was. I set rules that he wouldn't follow, and he started getting into all kinds of trouble in school. The principal called me to come in many times, and he would tell me he had missed classes, gotten into a fight, or was hanging out with students who were involved with drugs. When I confronted Albert, he would talk back. I didn't have the patience to listen to him, and I got angry instead. We started fighting and arguing constantly, as he kept breaking the rules that I set.

I was so worried about whether he was taking drugs, and how that could ruin his life. The thought of this terrified me; I felt I had to do something about the situation.

When he was thirteen, I decided to send him to a boarding school in England, hoping that in a different environment away from home, he would do better. And I thought that after all, I had grown up in England too.

I, of course, didn't go there by force, I didn't go alone, and I didn't have a broken family, at least not in the same way.

At this time, I didn't think about what my son was going through inside of him—he had divorced parents, his father had just disappeared from his life, and his mother didn't know how to cope with any of this. He was going through his own teenage years, and everything was magnified in his life. I see it more clearly now. Rebellion was the only way to release his confusion and anger. How did I not feel for him? What kind of mother had I become? Just the thought of this now makes me feel ashamed.

At the time, my focus was on his behavior, keeping him away from drugs and out of trouble, and I hoped boarding school would be the answer.

The day we arrived in a little town called Malvern in Worcestershire, it was almost evening. We checked into a small bed-and-breakfast and went out for dinner at a local restaurant. Both of us were quiet. We ate our dinner and went back to the hotel.

Later that night, I ran a hot bath for myself and while I was soaking in the tub, I started crying uncontrollably, sobbing. I covered my mouth to avoid making too much noise.

My heart was aching. I had never felt so hopeless in my life.

My boy was leaving me, and nothing would be the same anymore.

When I went back home, I continued to feel a lot of guilt and sadness around leaving Albert. I continued to struggle with my lack of confidence.

Frank continued to be very patient with me, gently encouraging me to try this or that. He said it didn't matter what it was, even if it was just to find a hobby; he would support me fully.

I was ashamed to let him down again, especially after that session with the psychologist. But I couldn't bring myself to do anything.

Then one day he came home and told me his friend Max was looking for someone to head up a headhunting business in Shanghai, China. Frank thought it would be a good opportunity for me, that I should go talk to him. "You have so much experience in doing start-ups," he said. "This should be a good fit for you. And you can always learn something new."

The voice in my head was resisting, saying I had never done this sort of business before, and I didn't have the skill to do it. Besides, I thought, headhunting wasn't my interest. It wouldn't work. I kept finding all the reasons why I couldn't do this, but he kept telling me to go, just to talk. He was trying to help me, I knew, as he'd tried to do so many times. He was always so patient, always encouraging me without judgment, only love and care. And I couldn't remember how many times I had said no to him about something like this.

Now this time, I wanted to say no again. But I no longer wanted to keep hurting him and disappointing him.

I couldn't do that to him anymore. I decided I would go, just to talk.

I was afraid to step out—terrified. The voices were still there, self-doubt was still pulling me back, but I was now fighting to break loose. It was like a tug-of-war this time, and I pushed myself out of the door to face the demon.

I was sick of the way I had been behaving. It wasn't me. I felt like no matter what the outcome of the day was, it wouldn't be worse than where I already was.

The day of the meeting, I went to my wardrobe, took out a black business suit that I hadn't worn for years, then put on some simple jewelry to make myself look more presentable.

As I walked into the office building in Central, my heart was pounding. I saw men and women in their beautiful attire, looking professional and confident, and I felt I didn't belong there. I felt scared, something I had never felt before in such a situation. It wasn't a pleasant feeling. But I had promised Frank I would meet Max, and I couldn't turn away now; it wouldn't be right.

I went up to the office where the secretary showed me to a meeting room and told me Max would be there shortly. As I was waiting, I felt so uncomfortable. I was sure it showed on my face. Everyone would see it. The fear was strong, but I couldn't do anything about it—at this point, I couldn't leave. I felt trapped. It was a horrible feeling.

The door opened and Max walked in, smiling. I shook his hand, and he asked about Frank. I replied he was doing well.

Our conversation was casual. We talked about travelling, his work, a little about our kids, his wife, and Frank; I began to relax a little. He then asked about my experience and I told him what I had done in the past for my family and Gary's family. The construction business in Brunei. Handling the sultan palace project. Starting the trading business in Hong Kong. Bringing the carpet mill from trading to a full integrated plant in China. The animal feed mill plants. My work for Gary's business. All my experience setting up new businesses and doing business in Hong Kong, China, and the US.

As I talked, I could feel my voice start to change. I was more comfortable and at ease; I was surprised to hear my own voice talking about it.

It was indeed me who had done all that work before—I could feel it in my body. I had relived those moments of my life as I was talking. The images had appeared in front of me.

I could feel my face relax. The fear was no longer as strong.

I sat up taller in the chair as we continued talking for almost an hour. As Max asked more questions about my experience, I was able to continue on with some pride in me for what I had done. I left the office with a sense of having just found myself again. It was a strange feeling, but it sure was a good feeling. I felt like a big stone had been lifted from my shoulder.

Over the years, the fear in me had become so powerful, it consumed me and stopped me from trusting my own ability. It made my whole body tighten up; my face was tense most of the time.

I had always had financial support from my family in my business work, and so I thought all my success was because of that. Added to this was something my mother had once told me. She was a superstitious person—she believed in fortune-telling—and because of a fortune that was read, she once told me I would not be able to take the first chair in the company. I was only good at execution, but not leading. I would only follow. Even though I didn't agree with her and argued with her, that voice was there to remind me that I was not good enough. That sense of not being good enough came back when my marriage didn't work and when my father wouldn't allow me to handle the project.

On my own, I could have found a job, started a new business, done something, but this belief that I wasn't good enough stopped me. It was all my mind could focus on. "You are not enough on your own. You can never be what you want to be without your family."

Once I began having financial difficulties, I had been afraid to let my friends see the truth of it. I thought if they knew I no longer had the financial means to do things, they might laugh at me, or even distance themselves from me. The feeling of shame was overwhelming. Along with my belief that I wasn't enough without my family, it devasted my sense of self-worth.

Meeting Max helped me see that money had helped me for sure, but I hadn't given myself any credit for my own ability. When I left the family business, I felt like a part of me was lost in the split too. Now, I was finally realizing it wasn't true and that it didn't happen that way. I am still who I am, I thought. I've got it in me. All I need to do is believe in myself.

I went into the meeting expecting to come away feeling ashamed and inadequate. But it didn't turn out that way, and I realized those feelings only existed in my head, as part of the fear that had consumed me. Trying to avoid confronting the fear had kept me from wanting to do anything. When I was willing to face the demon, step into the place of deepest vulnerability that I dreaded, it started to lose some of its power.

It was a small win, but an important first step. It gave me the courage to know I could do this. It pushed me forward.

I went home and told Frank about the meeting. I was talking fast, eager to let out this joy that I hadn't felt for a long time. He listened attentively as I spoke and I could feel his happiness for me, seeing me slowly coming out of my shell. Frank is a beautiful man, and I wouldn't have done this without his love and support. I was and am forever grateful for that.

Two days later, I got a call from Max, who told me there was a lady from Taiwan named Emily who was looking for someone to start up a training business in Shanghai, China. She was only in Hong Kong for a day, and would I want to meet? I could hardly believe my own voice when I said "yes" without hesitation. My confidence was slowly coming back.

It was the love that I began to feel, as the driving force. I could call it courage, confidence, determination, or any number of names, but it came down to love. Not just from others, but more importantly, from myself. It was self-love.

When I confronted my fears of not being good enough, things began to change. When I started to really see and believe in myself again—looking at what was inside me instead of just at what I saw as my failures—I could start to feel it. It wasn't based on others seeing me in a certain way or needing to be perfect. It started to grow beyond that.

Frank had showed me how it was possible to love unconditionally. I hadn't known this could exist, because I had never experienced receiving love without judgment. My parents loved me the way they knew how, but they didn't know how to express it. Their way of showing love was subtle, by doing things for us and by giving us material things. We never talked about love. This was simply how they had been raised as part of a traditional culture. But it left me with a sense of not receiving real love, even though I knew they had always loved me. I grew up feeling I needed to earn it—to please and obey and succeed. Frank taught me how to be loved in a way that felt unconditional. And so when my self-love started to grow, it felt less conditional too.

This seed of self-love was what started to bring back my confidence and brought me back to the real meaning in life. It brought me back to being able to give love to others more unconditionally. Giving is the most beautiful thing in life, and when there is no expectation in the giving, it finds its truest, most meaningful form. That is where the fulfillment comes from.

That was exactly what I wanted. A fulfilling life!

I took the job with Emily in the training and consulting business, and Frank and I moved to live in Shanghai. Eventually she and I became very good friends.

This was the first job of its kind I ever worked outside of my family business. All I knew was to run it like my own, much like what I did for my family, so I did. The only difference this time was I was doing it without the support of my family, which I previously depended on so much.

This was an amazing feeling—knowing what I could do, proving to myself that I was capable of doing anything I put my heart into. It was the start of a new chapter, a wonderful new chapter. And it was possible because Frank believed in me, at a time when I couldn't believe in myself. The unconditional love he had for me led me to face my fears, and then I could start to let them go. Then I could see the truth.

That I could believe in myself. That I was worthy of love. And that not loving and believing in myself had been the only thing that had been stopping me.

Chapter 8

UNCONDITIONAL LOVE

Our move to Shanghai marked the beginning of a new chapter for me, a return to a fulfilling sense of purpose and direction. I loved the challenges. I was working in a new field centered on training and self-awareness—I was learning so much, about the field and myself—and also living in a new country. It was an exciting time. During this period, though, things continued to be difficult for Albert, and that weighed heavily on me. Because of my work, I also began to have a different perspective. I started to see my parenting in a new light, with a new awareness. I began to question some of my beliefs around parenting that didn't seem to be working.

I saw I had been parenting just as my parents (and their parents) had done, and I wanted to break the pattern.

When I look back to my own childhood, my parents were too busy with their work to find time to teach us much about life beyond duty and the business. They did what they could and prayed that we turned out alright. They were loving and caring parents, showing affection and love their subtle and never verbal way. And I'm sure they worried about my brothers and me all the time. But they certainly were never connected to my siblings' and my emotional experience, and while they absolutely loved me, I didn't always feel it when I needed it most.

We learn so much from our parents without being consciously aware of it, and I had realized I was doing the same thing with my own son. I didn't know how to show Albert how much I loved him—I had always kept most of the feelings inside of me, thinking my son would know it, that he would be alright. It wasn't until I became more aware of my own feelings, and my longing for my parents' love and approval, that I saw my actions and inactions could be creating the same ache in Albert.

In the years following the divorce, I was fighting my own demons. I didn't know how to take care of him emotionally while I was totally lost in my own world.

Once he went to boarding school in England, all I did was send money for his tuition and living, and occasionally go visit him. He was struggling in school—now attending a new school in Cambridge—and when he would visit us in Shanghai during the summer, he seemed angry most of the time. For a long time, I didn't know what to do, and so I did nothing except worry.

But two years after I started my new chapter in Shanghai, I was in a different frame of mind. I had gained back my own confidence. In addition, the last few years of my career had brought new growth to my life. Not only because it marked the start of a new chapter for me, but also because of the type of work I did. I worked for a consultant training company that did a lot of self-awareness training, and I would also go through this training. I learned a lot. It helped open up how I looked at things and helped me understand more about the human side of behavior.

I knew I had to do something, even if I didn't know exactly what or how to do it. I was determined. I couldn't let him go down a path that would ruin his future. I thought maybe my being closer to him would make things better, so I resigned from my job and boarded a plane to Cambridge.

I arrived unannounced one morning. When he opened the door, he didn't seem surprised to see me. "Did you have a fight with your husband?" he said coldly.

I was angry and surprised at his comment and manner. I replied with coolness of my own, but controlled my temper. I had come to help; I didn't want to fight. "Don't worry, I am not here to trouble you. I can take good care of myself. I have many friends in England and I will be alright."

I realized I was in for an uphill battle, but I was not going to give up. I could tell I needed help and thought that hiring a coach—a parenting coach—might give me some insight on how to work with my son.

I found a coach through a search online and we met for coffee. As we sat across from each other, I told her what had brought me to her. Then she looked in my eyes and got straight to the point.

"Do you love your son?" she asked.

I was surprised at the question. "If I didn't love him, I wouldn't be here asking for your help," I replied bluntly.

"It sounds like your love comes with a lot of conditions," she said. "When he doesn't do what you tell him, you make him feel he is not worth your love. Let me be honest with you. Your son is over eighteen years old—you have no control of him except financially." She continued. "How often do you praise your son?"

It took me a while to reply. "It all depends on how well he does—if he does well, I will praise him, of course." Her question got me thinking—when was the last time I praised him, or did I ever praise him? Wasn't that how I was raised? My parents never praised me—although they acknowledged it in their hearts—but when I did wrong, I sure would hear from them. I only received the criticism. I supposed this was the right way to parent.

"Here is your homework," she said. "I want you to at least find one thing to praise every day. We will meet again next week."

One week later, we met. She asked me how I did and I told her I couldn't find anything that was worth praising—I had no idea how to do it or even what it meant. To praise someone, in my mind, meant recognizing something extraordinary.

She couldn't believe I couldn't find a good thing to say to my son. I was ashamed but I really didn't know how to do it. So I asked her, "Could you show me an example?"

"You could say he looks good today, or you like something about the clothes he's wearing . . ."

I rolled my eyes. "He has five different colors in his hair and he wears those dropped hips pants. How can I praise that?"

"You just have to find something to praise. Just do it!" she said.

My old belief was blocking me, keeping me from being able to look at things in a different way. Enough to where I was struggling to make such a simple change. My mind was so sure this would go nowhere. But somehow, I was still able to ask myself—if I was not getting the results that I wanted, shouldn't I try something different?

So I did. And it was a turning point in my relationship with my son.

One morning I did praise him on how he looked. "I like your T-shirt, the colors match with your hair," I said.

He was totally shocked to hear that. He looked down to his shirt and then said softly, as if he almost couldn't believe what he heard, "Thank you!" After that, whenever I wanted help from him, doing chores in the house or going to the supermarket, I would say "thank you" to him. I stopped treating him like a young kid, and stopped criticizing him even when I might disapprove of the things he did. It took a while for me to change; sometimes I had to bite my tongue, but I was patient.

I stayed in Cambridge with Albert for six months. Things didn't shift right away, but gradually I began to see changes in him and us. We started to talk more, and the tension between us became less and less. I was slowly building the relationship with my son. I was no longer being judgmental about the things that he did, and most importantly, I respected him as an adult and not a child anymore. To do this, I just had to be willing to step out to the unknown, into unfamiliar and even scary territory. To accept how I had always assumed it should be—that because I was his mother and wanted him to do well, I knew better and had a right to judge—might not be the best thing. I am so thankful I took the small step to try something differently, to have an open mind, to look at things from his point of view instead of only from mine. If I had kept holding on to my ego as a parent, needing to control everything, every outcome, just because he is my son, I would never be able to have the beautiful relationship I have with him today.

This exercise of beginning to praise Albert had such power in shifting our relationship because it helped me to extend a sense of love. As I stopped criticizing and judging him so often, instead of feeling like he wasn't enough, he was able to feel, more and more, my unconditional love for him.

Again, it came back to unconditional love.

Chapter 9

REFLECTIONS ON THE JOURNEY

In the years since those months in Cambridge, a lot has happened.

My work has evolved in new directions and continued to be a meaningful part of my life. After working two years with Emily, I started a new leadership training and development consulting business with two partners, and over the next thirteen years, we built it into a multimillion-dollar business. We sold the company at the time of writing this book.

It was a great feeling knowing I accomplished something I never thought I would without financial help from my parents. The limiting belief and the little voice from my mother in my head that always told me I could never do it alone, that I could follow but not lead—it wasn't true.

My success didn't come without challenge, but it was always enriching challenge. With my confidence returning, I was able to see with new eyes. I was starting to believe life was not happening *to* me but *for* me, to continually lead me to the next level. I knew that everything I faced held an opportunity for growth, and my new work brought continually deeper awareness. When challenges came, I was able to push through. When I was able to look at things in an objective way and not let fear and doubt consume me, I was able to find a solution. I learned that instead of letting events defeat us, we can face them up front with an awareness they are there to make us grow, no matter how hard it might seem. And once we see things with this new meaning, we will have the confidence to fight on, to dance with our most challenging circumstances, and eventually we will overcome them. As a result, we will grow and learn and become a better version of ourselves.

Over the years, there have been continual challenges, continual growth, and continual blessings. But these experiences I've written of—learning to receive unconditional love, and to love myself and my loved ones without condition—are the most profound gifts of my life.

My relationship with Albert has continued to grow. Today, he and I often spend time sharing stories about the past. We laugh and cry when we talk about those we loved dearly who are no longer with us. We share sadness about what is unjust in the world and talk about our goals and purpose and how we commit to them. I've gotten to learn more about him and his years studying overseas; at times, I've been surprised at how little I knew of his past and what he had gone through. It's such a privilege to see who he is. We are the best of friends now, talking and exchanging messages every day. Encouraging each other to grow, I have to say. I am learning so much from him.

I now am willing to listen, trust, and have an open heart to see him as a person and not just as a child through the lens of a traditional Chinese family relationship. To see him grow into a man who has strong values, passion in what he does, and determination; who is kindhearted, believes in himself, is willing to put in the hard work, and loves others. All of who he is makes me feel so blessed to be his mother.

Al in China, doing what he loves with his music
- Shanghai, 2018

I believe in him and now trust that with love, he will always be alright. He will find the courage and strength he needs to overcome any obstacles life might bring. I want this more than anything in the world. Isn't it what all loving parents want for their children?

I've learned that when we put aside our need to control because we think we know best or have more experience and, instead, we love, we guide, we trust, we let go, our children will be alright. They will have more confidence in themselves, while knowing we will always be there to love them no matter what. Our love is the greatest fuel to their soul.

And while most parents love their kids, we don't always share our love in a way that lets our kids fully feel it.

In writing this book, I've been reflecting on the family journeys I've been a part of, as a child, as a mother, and as a spouse. My parents gave me their love the best way they knew how. They came from a traditional culture and believed it taught them the right way to raise their children—my mother even sacrificed her own happiness to do what she thought was right, for the sake of keeping harmony in the family. I had done the same at an early age too, staying in my marriage when I knew it wasn't working for me, and then leaving the family business. Instead of fighting for what I wanted in the business, I left to preserve the harmony and not risk losing the relationships with my brothers. I was afraid to lose the love.

My ex-husband, Gary, had lived in the same way. He married me just because his father wanted him to. He too was afraid of losing the love from his father, and his father, on the other hand, thought he knew what was right for him. Being obedient to his parents and putting the family first were more important than his own happiness.

We were all living with a long-held belief system that emphasized obedience to parents (because they knew best) and putting the family first over individual happiness.

In my culture and in many others too, our devotion to family is a big part of our lives, sometimes in beautiful ways. For instance, I grew up with deep respect and a sense of caring for others and particularly for the elderly—these are good values to have. Other values, such as always considering the needs of family members before our own, are sometimes limiting. When I finally realized some of these limiting beliefs were actually causing harm to me and not serving me, I knew I had to let them go.

When you let go of something so ingrained in you, it is a challenge.

My parents provided everything for us, they protected us from harm, and when we made mistakes, they helped us to solve the problem. This was done to such an extent that when they weren't around to protect us, sometimes we would feel totally lost, without an ability to fight, to find a solution to our problem, to stand back up when we fall, to have the courage to live the lives that we wanted. I was a good example of this. I thought I would be able to find my way when I left my marriage and the family business. I thought I was tough. But when things fell apart, I didn't have the confidence to stand back up right away because my parents were not there to hold my hand.

I had taken the step forward to make a change, but I did not anticipate the challenges and fear that would come with it. In those challenges and fear, I lost my confidence. I was filled with self-doubt, uncertainty about the future, and a need to protect my ego and how people saw me.

When Frank came along, he became my savior. When I was with Gary, I was unseen and not understood. With Frank everything was different. I could feel the love, an unconditional love, and I drank it in. I dumped all my negative energy into him, and he absorbed it without complaint. Then I realized how selfish I was being, always making our relationship all about me and not about us. I saw how much my behavior was hurting him and that he was suffering from it. Then I understood it was so wrong and I was ashamed. I was behaving like a victim, feeling sorry for myself, knowing what I wanted but unwilling to take responsibility. The values I had learned from my parents to respect and care for others helped wake me up. And Frank's unconditional love continued to hold me until I was able to fully step out of my fear and begin rebuilding my life and confidence again.

Frank's unconditional love gave me a new hope, a new life. As I began to open into life again, though, I was still struggling with Albert. I was making mistakes with my son that were similar to my own experience growing up, parenting from that same belief system that told me as the parent, I must always know best and he just needed to do what I told him. Once again I questioned my belief system and realized it wasn't serving me, or Albert. I needed to learn to let go, to trust his ability to take good care of himself, to believe in him, to love him unconditionally and encourage him to find his own destiny and have faith in himself. From there, we were able to build back the relationship that was lost. It started with my willingness to change as a parent, which eventually influenced him and gave him the confidence to find his own path.

When I was writing about my early relationship with my son, I called him one day to apologize for what I had done in those years. I hadn't thought about his feelings at the time of the divorce and afterwards, thinking he was still very young. Then I sent him away because I didn't know how to deal with his behaviors, instead of loving him and guiding him. I was hurting him without realizing it. He told me, "Mom, it wasn't your fault; you were going through a tough time." There is no excuse, but I still wanted him to know I am sorry. Being honest now is the right thing to do.

But in our culture, it is very rare to admit we are wrong. The belief that all our decisions are for the family gives us the excuse that they're all the right things to do.

Family continues to be precious to me. My own family, Frank and Albert, are important to me, as are my parents and my brothers. I love them all. In pursuing my own life, I never forgot the things that my parents taught me. They've continued to be the values that I live by, only now I am more aware of what values are important and what beliefs are not helping. The journey of discovery is ongoing. Growing is part of life; when we don't grow, we will die.

Having self-awareness was a big part of my growth.

I was lucky to have an opportunity to work for a company in the field of personal development. Instead of continuing living in my own small world, that work helped me open my mind to see things differently, to challenge my own beliefs and to try a new way when the old way wasn't working. All these require a new mindset of willingness to try, to step out to the unknown, to challenge the status quo and push myself forward rather than let fear consume me. This is part of growing.

Some of us are afraid to do new things so we settle for what is familiar, even if it brings suffering and pain. Sometimes we think we don't have any other choice. But this is based on fear. We do have choices to do things differently.

We all have challenges; even the most successful person on earth has challenges. How we deal with those challenges is what makes the difference. It is about love. We all need love in our relationships, in our life. At the end of the day, it is what matters the most.

Some cultures focus on the family and neglect individual needs, and some instead focus on individual needs, putting oneself first before anything else, but wouldn't it be a happier, more meaningful life if we could consider what we want and need and also include the love and care of our family? We don't have to choose from one or the other.

I just returned from spending three weeks with Albert in Orange County, California, where he now lives and works as a musician. He has been writing, producing, and performing his music since he was fourteen years old. It is his passion and love, and he wants to help others through it, which I think is a wonderful thing to do.

We spent a lot of time talking about work, family, his dreams, and life in general, and there were moments when I could feel his worry about the future, how he wasn't sure he was doing the right thing. I listened attentively, and occasionally, I would ask him a question about what his concern was. He told me the world has changed so fast he wasn't sure his music would still appeal to his young fans. And the music scene has changed so much ever since he returned from China three years ago. His focus is more around his journey of growth and love, and this is reflected in his music, and at times he's concerned with whether it will connect with a younger audience.

Al performing at the China Music Festival. He was one of the few Asian hip-hop artists at the time - ChengDu, China, 2019

Al's fans are his biggest supporters. He always put on a great show - Shanghai, China, 2017

Years ago, in a situation like this, our communication would have been challenging. I would very likely have told him to do this or to do that as if I knew exactly what was best for him, without considering his feelings of worry and fear. He would have resented my comments, thinking I was once again judging his ability to handle his work. We would have likely argued, with him telling me I knew nothing about music, and we would end our conversation with both of us feeling unhappy, hurt, and unheard.

Now our relationship is so different. I am no longer imposing my ideas or know-it-all attitude onto him. In conversations like these, I tell him how proud I am that he is my son. I tell him that I feel his fear and understand his worry, and thank him for sharing them with me. I tell him how much I believe in him and encourage him to do the same, because believing in oneself is one of the most important beliefs to be successful. We talk about his fear and obstacles he has encountered, and I ask how they've made him feel. Then I acknowledge what he's shared and assure him it is okay to have such feelings. Sometimes, I might suggest to him to look at his fears with a different eye, to talk to them with this different perspective. Like, "Mr. Fear or Mr. Worry, I know you are there to try to protect me, but instead of helping me, you stop me from achieving what I want to achieve. I have to let you go, because I know you're not real, and I know I would be alright without you."

It is a totally different relationship. I feel I am showing my son what possibility would look like without judging, without expectation, knowing he will find his path of success no matter what obstacles he faces. Most importantly, I am showing him love without judgment, and he knows he can trust and let his feelings be known. This is different from my own experience as a child.

When I was younger, I seldom told my parents how I felt, when I was worried or scared. Partly because I didn't want them to worry about me, but in reality, we had never had conversations where we freely shared our inner feelings. I was even ashamed to cry in front of my family. Growing up in a traditional family environment like this taught me to keep my feelings to myself, to find my own way through my emotional pain, to be strong in order to be loved by my family. I had received attention and approval for being a capable person, and that became part of how I felt loved.

My parents very seldom showed their vulnerability or talked about their own worries and concerns. We rarely talked about our emotions. We didn't talk about a lot of things, and certainly didn't talk deeply about things that mattered. They felt their job was to provide and to protect us, to teach us how to be strong, take responsibility, and be a good person. They passed these values on mostly through their own behavior and also by correcting ours. It did make me strong in ways, but at the same time, it made me long for their love even more because I felt I needed to earn it.

When I went through my divorce, I was afraid, I was lost, and most of all, I felt I was alone. My parents loved me but they didn't know how to communicate with me, and so they left me there to deal with it by myself, thinking I would be alright. The reality was that their absence at that time in my life devastated me. I felt like I was fighting a big battle on my own, without any help. It was a horrible feeling and it still hurts when I think about it. But I don't think my parents fully knew what I was going through. I didn't know how to communicate with them. Instead of sharing my pain with them, I stood strong in front of them because I didn't want to appear weak. Being strong had been a way of getting love and attention.

Ever since I left the family business and went through the divorce, our family relationships have had more distance. For years, we didn't talk as much or spend as much time together as we had before, and at times, I even felt I didn't as fully belong. In recent years, we've become more present again in each other's lives, and this has meant a lot to me. I have always loved them very, very much. And I've always known they loved me. There is still some pain, though, around aspects of how that love was communicated and received.

I certainly didn't want my son to feel the same way. I did repeat the same patterns when he was young, but now I know what it feels like to be loved unconditionally and I don't want to make the same mistakes again. I no longer want to simply be right. I want to care, to love, and more than that, to show that love in a way it can really be felt.

I have seen so many people suffering from difficulties in their relationship with their children. They feel helpless and don't know what to do. I was once in this situation too. There was no miracle overnight, but each step I took, things became better and better. I just had to be willing to take the first step and do things differently.

As parents, we all love our children—there is nothing more painful than seeing your child in pain and yet not being able to help them. And sometimes we want to be able to fix things. But I've realized that help with money or materials or solutions isn't the most important thing. For a child, what is essential is getting and feeling the love they need and deserve from their parents. The most essential thing is for them to know you love them, that you are always there to love them no matter what fear comes to knock on their doors. The power of unconditional love will help them find their own solutions, help build their confidence, and help them believe in themselves and love others.

Centering on unconditional love makes so much else possible. And more than that, love and connection are the key to a beautiful relationship and a beautiful life. Without them, life is hollow. They belong in the center of everything.

My journey has taught me this, and I hope to pass on this truth through the gift of my life.

During one of my many visits to see Al in California - Anaheim, US, 2022

Our happy family - Anaheim, US, 2022

ACKNOWLEDGMENTS

I want to thank my husband, Frank, for showing me what love is. Thank you for loving and believing in me.

I want to thank my mother and my father for all the love and the opportunities. They helped make me who I am.

I want to thank my son, Albert. You are my inspiration. Thank you for encouraging me to write this book.

I want to thank all my siblings, Mike, Barry, and John. I appreciate you each being in my life.

I want to thank Don and Janie Dunlap for their love. It means a lot to me.

I want to thank EVERYONE I've met in my life who has made a positive impact on me. You know who you are.

I would also like to thank Stacy Ennis, who taught me how to write by providing a structure and easy-to-follow process, and also encouraged me when I had doubts about being able to write this book. My thanks to my editor, Robin Bethel, who worked very hard to smooth my English and helped me to bring this book alive without losing the originality.

Finally, I would like to thank my ex-husband, Gary, and his family. Without that chapter of my life, I wouldn't be who I am today.

ABOUT THE AUTHOR

May *Lam Rocco* was born in Hong Kong to a very traditional Chinese family. After leaving her family business, she successfully built and sold a leadership training and development consulting company in China. She is now dedicated to promoting relationships between parents and children and helping others build their confidence. Having previously lived in Hong Kong, Brunei, Taiwan, the UK, and China, she currently splits her time between the United States and Asia.

NOTES IN CLOSING

If you enjoyed this Memoir, please consider leaving a review wherever you discovered and bought the book. Reviews are the lifeblood of independent authors, and can often make an enormous difference in how successful we are at making sure our stories are read or heard by the people who need them most. We would be incredibly grateful for your help in sharing this story as far and wide as possible.

To receive more information about how to heal your relationship with your children/parents, visit.....

https://linktr.ee/maylamrocco or scan the QR code below.

Thank you for reading.

May Lam Rocco

Scan me